No Cooking At All.
Almost. Hardly.

No Cooking At All.
Almost. Hardly.

by Tukey Koffend

With Illustrations by the Author

SUNSTONE
PRESS

SANTA FE

Photograph of author by Audrey Topping

Sunstone books may be purchased for educational, business, or sales promotional use. For information please write: Special Markets Department, Sunstone Press, P.O. Box 2321, Santa Fe, New Mexico 87504-2321.

Library of Congress Cataloging-in-Publication Data:

Koffend, Tukey, 1921-
    No cooking at all—almost—hardly / by Tukey Koffend ;
illustrated by the author.
        p. cm.
    Includes bibliographical references and index.
    ISBN 0-86534-443-4 (pbk. : alk. paper)
    1. Quick and easy cookery. I. Title.

TX833.5.K645 2004
641.5'55—dc22
                                        2004017713

Published in

WWW.SUNSTONEPRESS.COM
SUNSTONE PRESS / POST OFFICE BOX 2321 / SANTA FE, NM 87504-2321 /USA
(505) 988-4418 / ORDERS ONLY (800) 243-5644 / FAX (505) 988-1025

Contents

Introduction

When I was growing up in Omaha we had rather unusual dinners on the nights when Florence, our cook, went out. On Thursdays my mother produced fried mush (which Florence had made before she left on her day off). Mother gave it to us swimming in maple syrup. and my sister and I loved it. Mother had one other specialty—in fact, the only other thing she knew how to make—chocolate ice box pudding with Hershey bars and lady fingers. We loved that even more! (I wish I had the recipe now). Sunday nights my father was chef, and he concocted what he called "Cheese Dreams," which were really just toasted cheese sandwiches with Durkee's. Sometimes we went to the popcorn stand and bought bags of fresh popcorn, which we ate in bowls with cream. Yum! No other kids we knew had that delicious treat for supper.

With this non-gourmet past I probably shouldn't be writing a cookbook at all, but somehow in the last 40 years I have learned something about cooking. I usually choose the easiest recipes, shy away from those with a long list of ingredients, and try to have things that need the same oven temperature or even better, take the same time to cook … like balsamic chicken and tomato and onion tart. Both go in a 350 degree oven for an hour. I cheat a lot, and use frozen spinach for spinach soufflés, frozen piecrusts and packaged mixes … things like that.

Much Too Long

$\mathcal{S}$imple food, yes but I like to dress up the dining table, and I have a stash of little objects to use...sugar animals from Mexico's Day of the Dead, Japanese toys, or small wooden carved animals, called alebrijes, from Oaxaca. And always flowers and candles.

So this is a cookbook for cooks like me—those who like to entertain but don't want to spend the whole day in the kitchen getting ready. We call ourselves lazy, but secretly think we are rather clever, for we can actually produce unusual and tasty dishes with very little effort.

Here's your chance to learn some of our sneaky secrets!

Hints For A Dinner Party

Hints For A Dinner Party

It's no fun to be frantic and frenzied when entertaining. Some simple tips for an organized entertainment:

TABLE

You can set the table the night before the party or in the morning. Try to make things look festive and welcoming with flowers, either in a nice bowl or in three or four little vases, lots of votive candles, and maybe a few of your favorite small treasures. Colorful placemats are fun.

NAPKINS

The bigger the better, and I like them poufed up in napkin rings. Maybe the flowers will match the napkins?

GLASSES

Dinky little wine glasses don't seem very gracious. Use big (but not enormous) goblets which will do for either white or red wine. If you want to serve water, use more goblets.

A Dinky Little Glass

SILVER AND SALT

Put out the silver: knives right, spoons outside them; forks, left, with first course forks far left and dinner ones in next to the plate. (One eats outside-in.) Put two salt cellars (see special recipe below) and two pepper grinders on the table for eight or more guests.

PLACE CARDS

It's is always nice to have what the French call a placement and you can easily make some name cards on colored paper or print them in a fancy font with your computer.

COFFEE

Measure it out and have it ready to go. Put the cups, saucers, sugar bowls, and cream pitcher to be filled later, on a tray…all ready for the last minute.

ET CETERA

Get out the serving bowls, platters, etc. Check the ice, put the white wine in the fridge, open the red and recork gently before the guests are expected.

A Very Important Recipe

Our Special Salt

Our Special Salt is a MUST for almost any salad, as well as for hundreds of other dishes. Dr. Alex Gancarz, a VIP at the Los Alamos National Lab, and a very good chef—too good to be called just a cook—gave me the recipe a few years ago, and I have been making it, using it on everything, and giving it away, ever since.

> 1 cup coarse sea salt
> zest of 2 lemons
> 3 garlic cloves
> 3 tablespoons chopped rosemary

In blender place two minced garlic cloves, rosemary, salt, and lemon zest and whirr a minute or two until mixed but not pulverized. Put it in a glass jar with a lid, poke the third garlic clove, halved, down into the mixture, and let sit for three or four days before decanting into small shakers.

Hors D'oeuvres and Canapes

All my dictionaries give more or less the same definition of canapé: "a cracker or a small piece of toast spread with cheese or meat and served before a meal." Hors d'oeurves definition is about the same: "a preparation served before a meal to stimulate the appetite". I thought appetizer meant "first course" but it's the same as hors d"oeuvres and canapé, so our former "Appetizer" chapter is now called "First Course."

A really indolent hostess might make do with olives, nuts and cheese for canapés, but here are some recipes for producing more appealing tidbits with very little trouble. It's important to serve bite-size finger food so the guests won't dribble down their fronts or onto your rug.

Two of the easiest, and the biggest successes, at my house, have been cheese melts and won ton crisps. Guests always wonder where I got them and then, what's in them. They are SO simple that I am proud to share their secrets.

CHEESE MELTS

I had these first in Kansas City at Ellen and Irv Hockaday's house; she used Monterey Jack, and sliced it very thin. They are very delicate and delicious. Or you can go the easy route and buy grated cheese in baggies at the store. For either method you need a really heavy non-stick baking pan, or pan liners called Silpats, which will keep any cheese from sticking. These cheese melts are even good right out of the freezer.

Heat oven to 350 degrees.

> **a bag of grated Cheddar, Mozzarella,**
> **Monterey Jack, or mixed cheeses**
> **cayenne pepper**

With your fingers, pluck about a tablespoon of cheese and make little oval piles about three inches by one inch on the pans, placing them about an inch apart. Sprinkle lightly with pepper if you want a bit of spice. Put in the oven where they will bubble and melt; after about five minutes peek in and see if the bubbles are diminishing, the wafers look fairly solid, and are only slightly brown. They are easily removed with a spatula.

WON TON CRISPS

No one ever guesses the ingredients in these delicious wafers.

Heat oven to 375 degrees.

> **Parmesan cheese, grated or shredded**
> **1/2 cup butter, melted**
> **package of won ton wraps**

These packaged Chinese wraps are usually found in the produce section of your grocery store. Leave the small wraps whole; cut large ones into four long pieces.

Brush the skins with butter, (I use a one-inch paint brush), and place them close together on a baking sheet, then sprinkle on a generous smattering of cheese.

Bake for 5 or 6 minutes, keeping a wary eye on them lest they start to burn. Let them get a light brown, not too dark. They last a long time in the freezer.

CHEESE/CRAB DIP

This is a wonderful dip for a big party. Do not be put off by the humble Velveeta!

2 pounds Velveeta cheese
2 cans drained crabmeat
1 can chopped pimientos
dash white pepper
French bread

Heat all the above in the top of a double boiler, stirring till blended. It is best served in a chafing dish with the bread for dipping. You may halve the ingredients for a smaller group.

ANCHOVY EGGS

hard boiled eggs
canned flat filets of anchovy
paprika

Boil the eggs for 10 or 12 minutes and cool under cold water; crack a few times, and peel them now or later. Half a hard-boiled egg is hard to eat with cocktails; these will be cut into thirds, so figure out how many you need for your guests. Cut anchovy strips into pieces about an inch and a half long. (Scissors are good for this task). Cut the eggs the long way carefully into thirds, drape the anchovy strips over them, once vertically and once horizontally, sprinkle with a little oil from the anchovy can, and add some paprika.

CHINESE DRUMETTES

Drumettes, the meaty part of chicken wings, are labeled as such at most grocery stores. Being rather gooey, they are better served on small paper plates at a "cocktail buffet".

Heat oven to 375 degrees.

> **2 packages drumettes**
> **8 tablespoons soy sauce**
> **4 tablespoons sesame oil**
> **tablespoon minced ginger**
> **4 or 5 tablespoons brown sugar**
> **1/2 cup honey**

Mix the soy sauce, oil, and ginger, and marinate chicken in the mixture in a glass baking pan for four hours or more. When ready to cook, drain off most of the marinade, cover the drumettes with the honey and then the brown sugar, bake for 20 minutes and put under the broiler for another five, turning the chicken as needed.

Being Rather Gooey

CREAM CHEESE

My sister and I always had tiny cream cheese and jelly sandwiches for our dolls' picnics when we were little. Here are some more sophisticated notions for cream cheese.

> **chopped and seeded cucumbers**
> **chopped tomatoes**
> **anchovy paste**
> **chopped olives**
> **red or black roe caviar**
> **sautéed mushrooms**
> **Roquefort cheese**

All lend themselves nicely to the endive, the celery or as a spread for crackers. Don't forget our Special Salt.

FILLED ENDIVE LEAVES or CELERY STICKS

Lots of things are good in endive leaves; stuffed they make a good first course, too. Stuff celery sticks with any of these mixtures, or spread it on bread. Here are a few ideas.

LUCIA'S NUTS

I know I said something scornful about nuts at the beginning of this section, but these are special. Lucia Watson is the owner and chef of Lucia's Restaurant in Minneapolis, and these nuts are in her cookbook *Savoring the Heartland*. They are very spicy; you might want to go easy on the cayenne and the pepper.

Heat oven to 350 degrees.

> **3 cups pecan or walnut halves**
> **1/2 stick butter**
> **1 tablespoon cinnamon**
> **1 teaspoon cayenne**
> **2 teaspoons white pepper**
> **1 teaspoon allspice**
> **1/2 teaspoon salt**
> **2 teaspoons sugar**

Spread nuts on a cookie sheet and toast for fifteen minutes. Trust your nose; they will begin to smell nutty and toasty.

Melt butter over low heat, put the toasted nuts in a large bowl and toss with the butter. Add the other ingredients and toss until well coated. Spread them onto a cookie sheet to dry.

PRETEND PATÉ

This recipe is from Ann Watson, "hostess with the mostess" in Aspen, Colorado. Ann is the mother of the restauranteur Lucia Watson. There are always dozens of yummy canapés at her cocktail parties.

> **1 package liverwurst sausage**
> **1 package vegetable paté**
> **1 1/2 jigger bourbon or brandy**

Mix and let sit in sunny place until warm enough to blend. (If it's not a sunny day, put the mix in a 200 oven, turn off the heat and let sit for ten minutes or so.) Good on crackers or toast. You may add chopped chives or a tiny bit of chopped mint.

QUESADILLAS (Microwave or Grilled)

flour tortillas
Monterey Jack or Cheddar cheese
finely chopped scallions
salsa

You may add chopped leftover chicken if you have some on hand.

Put a tortilla on a plate suitable for the microwave, layer it with plenty of cheese, a few chopped onions, a little bit of salsa and cover with another tortilla. Put a second pair on top of the first. You can do two quesadillas at a time in the microwave for 60 seconds. Cut each tortilla into small pie-shape slices. Two quesadillas should be more than enough for eight people.

For a crisp snack you may grill these same filled tortillas in a hot frying pan (no oil) and cut them into little squares.

Quesadillas, Ole!

SAUSAGE IN PASTRY

This comes from Laurel Laliberte, lovely wife of our favorite artist, Norman Laliberte. They live in Nahant, Massachusetts. Laurie's food is not only good but also beautiful. Even when serving her young son and his friends her presentations are adorned with flowers or shiny leaves.

Heat oven to 350 degrees.

> **1 package Pillsbury Crescent Roll Mix**
> **1 medium size beef or pork sausage**
> **egg yolk**

Boil the sausage for eight minutes. Roll out the crescent roll mix, and enclose the sausage in it. Seal the edges thoroughly with the egg yolk. Bake for 12 minutes; slice rather thickly and serve warm.

First Courses

CANTELOUPE WITH TARRAGON

I recently visited two young friends, John and Jessie Gordon, at their wonderful house on the river in Twin Lakes, Colorado, over Independence Pass from Aspen. They built the house themselves, as well as a mud-floored chapel with stained glass windows from Jessie's parents, Fritz and Fabi Benedict. John has a huge studio for his many projects, and Jessie has a sort of old mining-building studio for her neon work.

I could meander on about them for pages, but this is a COOK book, not an architectural critique. Jessie served this cantaloupe dish for dinner. Be sure you have a very, very, very, sharp vegetable peeler before attempting!

> **one cantaloupe…not too ripe**
> **juice of two limes**
> **small bunch of fresh tarragon**

Halve the cantaloupe and cut each half into six sections and use a vegetable peeler to slice off thin slices from end to end. Put the slices in piles on a platter and dribble lime juice over them. snip off the tarragon leaves, chop them, and scatter them about. Chill until serving time when you may arrange the slices artistically on plates.

CELERY ROOT REMOULADE

My recipe card for this obviously has seen a lot of use—it is spotted, torn and almost dark brown. I used to serve this dish often, but had forgotten all about it until it somehow surfaced from my recipe file; it was like seeing an old friend...a rather demanding old friend.

Don't be alarmed if your hands turn a sickly yellow after peeling and cutting the celery knob. You might want to wear gloves, or be prepared to wash up vigorously.

> **2 medium celery knobs**
> **3/4 cup mayonnaise**
> **1 tablespoon Dijon mustard**
> **1/12 tablespoon lemon juice**

Pare the celery knobs well...this is hard work. Cut them into slices about one-sixteenth of an inch thick and then into strips as thin or thinner than toothpicks.

Combine the mayonnaise, mustard and lemon juice. Add the celery sticks and chill until serving time.

A few crackers might be a nice addition.

Serves 6 (I think).

EEK! Yellow Hands!

CHICKEN SALAD

> roast chicken
> small red onion
> a few sticks of celery
> 1 cup mayonnaise
> juice of 1 1/2 limes
> lettuce leaves

Coarsely chop the chicken, red onion and celery. Mix with mayonnaise and lime juice. Add more mayo if necessary. The red onion and lime makes this chicken salad mix tasty. Serve the salad wrapped in lettuce, two portions per plate.

CHOPPED PINK SHRIMP

    1 pound shrimp
    1/2 cup mayonnaise
    3 tablespoons ketchup
    dash Chinese hot oil
    dash of pepper
    18 endive leaves

Boil the shrimp until they turn pink; drain, and let cool in their liquid. Mix the mayonnaise, ketchup, oil, and pepper. Peel and chop the shrimp and stir them into the sauce. Chill.

Put the mixture in endive leaves, three leaves for each guest, arranged on small plates for a first course.

COLD EXOTIC SPINACH

A wonderful and unusual first course! We have always called it "Pittsburgh, 1919" because that is where and when it was served to my mother. Alas, as I said earlier, she was not much of a cook, but she had somehow remembered these ingredients. It's one of my favorite recipes and I don't think you will see it in any other cookbook.

Some people think this dish sounds disgusting, so you might not announce what it is made of until everyone is smacking their lips with pleasure.

> 3 cans spinach
> 2 cans sardines, drained
> 2 cans anchovies (drained) or 8 inches anchovy
>   paste
> 5 hardboiled eggs
> 1 cup mayonnaise
> 1/4 cup milk or cream
> 10 rounds of toasted bread or Melba toast

Drain (squeeze!) the spinach. Put it with the sardines and anchovies in a blender or Cuisanart, mix well and chill. Stir mayonnaise with milk till smooth; chill covered. About an hour before serving, make 10 little mounds of the spinach with an ice cream scoop onto a bread board.

Peel the eggs. If they are to be adornments, gently make a small cut lengthwise to extract the yoke without demolishing the whites. Cut the yolk in half, put one half on top of each spinach mound. Cut the white into narrow strips and drape them around the base of the mounds. You may skip this task if you wish, but do use the yolks.

Put the toast rounds on plates, top with the spinach mounds and slather each with a very large dollop of the mayonnaise mixture.

The last time I served this I cut the toast into small pieces before putting the spinach on it...no knives were needed and it was much easier for the guests to deal with.

Serves 10

PAMPLEMOUSSE ET CRABE (GRAPEFRUIT AND CRAB)

When (if!) you are invited to one of the small dinners of James Salter and his wife, Kay Eldredge in Aspen or Sagaponack, you know you will have an interesting meal with interesting people.

The Salters are dedicated and venturesome cooks.

The author of many novels, the screenplay of *Downhill Racer*, and a brilliant memoir *Burning the Days*, Jim received the Pen Faulkner award in 1989. He and Kay have collaborated on a new book, *Life is Meals* published by Callaway.

They devised this recipe based on a first course they had at a restaurant called Cuisinato in the French town of Fleurance. "Unfortunately," says Kay, "the restaurant no longer exists."

> **grapefruit halves (one per person)**
> **ripe avocado**
> **crab meat, fresh or canned**
> **"Russian" dressing of mayonnaise and ketchup**
> **red or black lumpfish caviar**

Empty the fruit from the grapefruit and cut into bite-sized pieces. Peel avocado and cut into bite-sized pieces. Mix the grapefruit, avocado and crabmeat. Serve in the empty grapefruit halves topped with the dressing and a dollop of red or black caviar.

Serves 6

SALMON WITH MUSTARD DILL SAUCE

>1 package of smoked salmon, coarsely chopped
>4 tablespoons mustard
>3 tablespoons sugar
>1 garlic clove, chopped
>2 tablespoons white vinegar
>1 cup vegetable oil.
>3 tablespoons chopped dill
>loaf cocktail rye bread

In a bowl mix mustard, sugar, garlic, and vinegar; then with a wire whisk slowly beat in the oil; add dill, then the salmon. Serve on slices of rye bread, topped with a dab of sauce. Or slice the salmon instead of chopping it and serve with sauce.

Soups

$\mathcal{I}$n looking over my collection of soup recipes, I found many that I had never used. Out they went! All were all too complicated (for me, at any rate) with too many ingredients. Here are some that made the cut.

COLD AVOCADO SOUP

        2 ripe avacados
        2 cans jellied consumme
        Our Special Salt, pepper
        1 teaspoon lemon juice
        dash Tabasco
        1/2 cup sour cream

Peel avocados and force through a sieve or gently whirr in a blender, Combine with cold unjellied consommé; add seasonings to taste. Chill 6 hours or overnight. To serve, divide among six bowls and top with sour cream.

COLD CHICKEN CURRY SOUP

This is a nice start for a summer luncheon.

> 2 cans of cream of chicken soup
> 2 cups cream or milk
> 2 tablespoons curry powder
> dash of fresh diced ginger
> chopped chives
> salt and pepper

Mix all the ingredients, except the chives, and chill for at least four hours. Garnish with chives before serving.

Serves 4

COLD POTATO SOUP

Phil and Pat Brown of Lake Okaboji, Iowa, gave me this recipe. I think they may have invented it? Anyway, it's easy and good.

>4 large potatoes
>3 cups chicken stock
>large onion, sliced
>1/2 pint yogurt, drained
>1/2 pint cream
>2 tablespoons pecans
>1 teaspoon lemon juice
>chopped chives

Boil the potatoes and onion in stock until tender, twenty minutes or so. ("Better Than Bouillon" makes a nice stock.) Drain. Put potatoes in blender with the pecans. Add yogurt, blend; add cream and lemon juice. Sprinkle with chives when serving.

JELLIED MADRILÈNE AND BURIED CAVIAR

    2 cans consommé madrilène
    2 tablespoons red or black caviar
    1/2 cup sour cream
    chopped chives

Chill the madrilène until jelled. Put a teaspoon of caviar in the bottom of a soup bowl, cover with consommé, add a generous dollop of sour cream and a few chives.

VICHYSSOISE

This is a simple version of the classic vichyssoise with peas instead of leeks, scallions instead of onions. Try a bit of curry if you like.

In *The Joy of Cooking* Irma Rombauer firmly admonishes her readers about the word vichyssoise "Yes," she says. "The last "s" is pronounced. Most Americans shun it in a 'genteel' way as though it were virtuous to ignore it." Well, maybe they don't speak French.

> 1 cup coarsely diced white potatoes
> 3/4 cup minced scallions
> 1 1/2 cup chicken broth
> 1 cup raw green peas
> 1/8 teaspoon curry powder
> 1 cup heavy cream
> 1 tablespoon chives

Heat potatoes, scallions and peas in the broth until it comes to a boil, then cover and cook ten more minutes until vegetables are barely tender. (If you are using frozen peas, put them in at the last minute.) Pour it all in the blender, add salt and curry powder; blend until smooth. Remove to glass bowl, stir in cream and refrigerate overnight. Serve sprinkled with chopped chives in soup bowls.

Serves 6

EASY BORSCHT/BORSCH

This Russian beet soup, spelled variously borscht or borsch, usually involves a lot of chopping and boiling. Here is a Santa Fe short cut from beautiful Jo Franzen, wife of Architect Ulrich Franzen.

> **1 can beets**
> **1 can tomatoes**
> **1 can onion soup**
> **1 can beef consommé**
> **1 jar pickled red cabbage**
> **sour cream**

Blend the beets, tomatoes, onion soup, consommé and cabbage. Chill. Serve topped with sour cream.

Serves 4

HOT CURRY SOUP

It's not reprehensible to use canned chicken soup and canned chicken for this soup.

1 can cream of chicken soup
1 can chicken broth
1 tablespoon curry powder
1/2 cup diced chicken
Major Greys Chutney

Heat soup, broth, curry powder and diced chicken in a heavy pan over moderate heat. Before serving add a spoonful of Chutney to each bowl of soup.

Serves 4

MULLIGATAWNY (sort of)

Kirt Pavitt, pianist with the Santa Fe Opera, described this soup, and when he offered to make it for me I had to be nice and say "Oh, do!" thinking to myself that it sounded horrid.

Not at all! I was wrong! It was delicious.

> **2 cans cream of chicken soup**
> **2 cans beef bouillon**
> **1 large jar or can of applesauce**
> **1 tablespoon curry powder**

Heat the soups, add the applesauce and the curry powder.

Serves 4

TOMATO/ORANGE SOUP

Talk about simple! But this has a very nice "mystery taste."

    2 cups orange juice, fresh or bottled
    2 cups cream of tomato soup

Mix. This may be served hot or chilled.

Serves 4

FOUR STAR MUSHROOM SOUP

Beverly Rhymes served this soup at her house in Santa Fe one night and it was the BEST. It's a bit more work than our other soups, but well worth the extra bother it entails.

> 1/2 cup butter
> 1/2 cup flour
> 1 1/2/ pound chopped mushrooms, mixed:
> wild (expensive) and regular (cheap)
> 3 tablespoons olive oil
> 1 onion, diced
> 5 cloves garlic, minced
> 1 teaspoon minced fresh rosemary
> 1 cup dry sherry
> 2 1/2 cups good vegetable or chicken stock
> 2 1/2 cups heavy cream
> 2 teaspoons minced oregano

First melt the butter in a small pan and stir in the flour gradually until it forms a thick paste and has a toasty aroma. Set aside.

Heat two tablespoons of the olive oil in a large heavy pan until hot. Save two cups of mushrooms for garnish, add the rest with the onion, half the garlic and rosemary and sauté these over medium heat about ten minutes until the mushrooms are tender and the onions lightly browned. Add the sherry, and boil to reduce by about half. Then add the stock and the cream. Keep the mixture at a simmer while adding the flour paste a large spoonful at a time. Stir with a whisk until blended after each addition. Keep adding flour until the soup is thick enough to coat the back of a spoon; you may not need to use all of it.

Pass the soup through a food mill or process it in small batches in a blender. It should be fairly smooth but retain a little texture. Season with Our Special Salt and pepper. Keep warm over low heat while you heat the remaining spoonful of oil to sauté briefly the rest of the mushrooms, garlic and oregano for garnish.

Ladle into bowls, topping with the sautéed mushrooms mix. You may want to add a dash more sherry to each bowl.

Stir Until It Coats The Back Of A Spoon

TURKEY CARCASS SOUP

I didn't like the term "carcass" but when my Thesaurus gave me "corpse" as an alternative I decided "Turkey Carcass Soup" sounded better than "Turkey Corpse Soup." Another Santa Fe recipe, this from my friend Jonathan Carleton.

> **turkey carcass/corpse**
> **3 or 4 quarts of water**
> **onion, halved**
> **carrot, halved**
> **1 cup barley**
> **2 cup sliced carrots**
> **2 cups diced onions**

Boil the turkey with the sliced onion and carrot in the water for half an hour; then remove the turkey and pick off and save any meat. Put the bones back in the water and boil another half hour. Let cool, skim off any fat, and now add the barley, sliced carrots, onions and turkey meat to the pot and cook another half hour on low heat. Season to taste.

Serve, refrigerate, or freeze in batches.

Salads

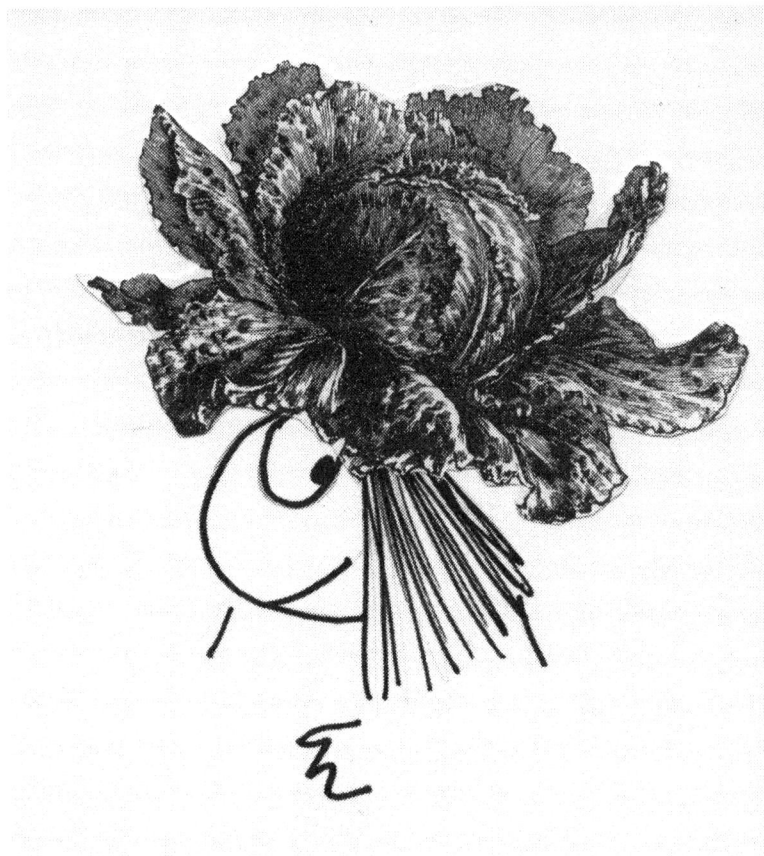

ARUGULA AND RED ONION SALAD

> 1 pound arugala
> large red onion, thinly sliced
> 2 pressed garlic cloves
> 4 tablespoons olive oil
> 2 tablespoons balsamic vinegar
> Our Special Salt and pepper

Rinse and drain arugula, mix with onion, garlic, oil and vinegar; add Our Special Salt and pepper.

BEET AND WALNUT SALAD

8 or nine medium beets
3/4 cup toasted walnut halves
6 tablespoons olive oil
3 tablespoons red wine vinegar
Our Special Salt and pepper
1/2 cup blue cheese
1/2 cup coarsely chopped Italian parsley
1 pear

Bake or boil the beets until tender but crisp, and slice into wedges, and let cool.

Combine oil, vinegar, salt and pepper.

Slice endive thinly and combine with cheese and parsley in large bowl.

Cut pear into quarters, removing core, and then slice into thin lengthwise slices; add it to endive, then add oil mixture and toss. Put the beets in and combine them gently.

CRAB SALAD

fresh, frozen or canned crabmeat
cucumber, coarsely chopped
tomato, thinly sliced
big bunch of chives, chopped
juice of one lemon
1 cup mayonnaise
1/2 cup sour cream

Combine crabmeat, cucumber, tomato, chives and lemon juice in glass bowl; add mayonnaise mixed with sour cream and chill well before serving.

GOAT CHEESE SALAD

3 tablespoons goat cheese with herbs
1/3 cup olive oil
1/8 cup rice vinegar
chopped Romaine or butter lettuce
Our Special Salt

With a spoon, break the cheese into the olive oil gently, then drizzle it onto lettuce; sprinkle with vinegar. Mix the salad lightly and be generous with Our Special Salt.

This salad may be enlivened with a handful of shelled pistachios.

PASTA SALAD

There was a sort of rage for pasta salads in the early nineties, but now one rarely sees them. Too bad. They should be brought back to favor; they lend themselves to all manner of ingredients and are very easy to create.

Don't refrigerate pasta salads.

> **cold cooked pasta in small fancy shapes**
> **olives**
> **scallions**
> **parsley**
> **basil**
> **tomatoes**
> **capers**
> **red or green peppers**
> **oil and vinegar dressing**
> **teaspoon sugar**

Mix any or all of the above and serve on small shreds of lettuce.

TUNA SALAD

2 cans good tuna
apple, chopped
handful of raisins
various nuts
cucumber, sliced
mayonnaise

Any of the above ingredients make a good tuna salad, If you are not using raisins, add some sliced scallions. Mix with lot of mayonnaise.

POTATO SALAD

You can be really creative with potato salad and add all kinds of embellishments: lots of green onions, chopped cucumbers or black olives. I think apples are vital for their nice crunch.

> 16 small red potatoes
> 1 cup mayonnaise
> 1 cup sour cream
> 1/2 cup half-and-half
> 12 scallions, sliced
> 2 apples, diced
> 2 cucumbers, peeled and sliced
> 2 stalks celery, diced
> 4 hard cooked eggs, sliced
> lettuce

Boil the potatoes for 20-25 minutes, covered, until done but not mushy, and drain them. Mix the mayonnaise, with the sour cream and half-and-half; add this to potatoes, scallions, apples, cucumbers, celery and eggs. Serve the salad in a large bowl lined with lettuce leaves and sprinkle generously with Our Special Salt and ground pepper.

Serves 8

Luncheon Dishes

*M*any years ago when I was a recent bride in Phoenix, my husband announced that he had invited Mr. and Mrs. Frank Lloyd Wright and a man called Dudley Field Malone to lunch. I knew who Mr. Wright was, of course, but had never heard of Dudley Field Malone. I found that he was one of Clarence Darrow's team of defense lawyers at the Scopes' trial and probably as well-known as Mr. Wright. It was a formidable guest list!

Looking through my meager collection of recipes and my only cookbook, I decided on a dish I hoped would be a success. I now reluctantly confess that it was a canned tuna fish casserole with crumbled potato chips on top, sort of a newlywed's special. The guests did not flinch, my husband did not file suit for divorce and Mr. Wright patted my knee under the table all during the meal.

Pitiful Hostess For Frank Lloyd Wright

Someone once said that a good party was made not by what was on the table but what was seated around it. Mr.Malone and the Wrights were charming guests.

Here are some better luncheon ideas, some of which work nicely as a side dish for a dinner party.

COLD CHICKEN AND NOODLES

This recipe calls for Somen, very thin Japanese noodles found in most grocery stores. Somen are also good cold, drizzled with soy sauce in small bowls

4 skinned and boned chicken breasts
1 package Somen

Poach the chicken breasts with water in a saucepan, cover and let simmer (not boil) for 30 minutes. Remove chicken and chill. Save a few tablespoons of the stock for the sauce.

Cook the somen in boiling water very briefly until it is limp, drain and let chill.

SAUCE

1/3 cup chunky peanut butter (optional)
3 tablespoons soy sauce
1 tablespoon sugar
2 teaspoons Chinese vinegar
5 tablespoons chicken broth
1 tablespoon minced garlic
I tablespoon minced ginger

Combine these ingredients in a blender and pour over chicken and noodles. Serve with a rather hearty salad.

CHINESE CHICKEN SALAD

I had this crispy, unusual salad years ago at the May Company restaurant near the County Museum in Los Angeles. Frying the rice sticks whilst preparing this is an exciting experience! They start out as innocent little transparent vermicelli and explode into what the Chinese call "Lion's Head." Don't be discouraged by so many ingredients.

> 1 pound skinless, boneless chicken breasts
> 1/2 cup chicken broth
> 2 cups vegetable oil for deep frying
> 1/4 pound Chinese rice sticks (dried rice vermicelli)
> 1/4 cup rice vinegar
> 1/2 cup sugar
> 2 tablespoons soy sauce
> 3/4 teaspoon dry mustard
> teaspoon minced fresh gingerroot
> head iceberg lettuce, shredded
> 1 cup chopped scallion, white and green parts
> 5 tablespoons almonds

Sliver the almonds and toast lightly in butter.

Simmer chicken in broth in a covered skillet for 1-5 minutes. Transfer to a plate, let it cool, and shred it.

In a large wok heat the oil to about 375 degrees and fry small handfuls of rice sticks for about 3 seconds on each side They will expand miraculously in volume instantly. Transfer with tongs to paper towels to drain.

Whisk the vinegar, sugar, oil, soy sauce, mustard and gingerroot together in a bowl until the sugar is dissolved.

In a large bowl combine lettuce, chicken, rice sticks and scallions and toss with the dressing.

Divide among six salad plates and sprinkle with the almonds.

DOODLET'S QUICHE

Theo Ruthling is the proprietor of "Doodlet's," a fascinating store in Santa Fe...full of books, treasures and trinkets. This is her version of an easy quiche.

Set oven to 350 degrees.

> 3 eggs
> 1/2 cup Bisquick
> 1/2 cup melted butter
> 11/2 cup milk
> salt
> 1 cup grated Swiss cheese
> 1/2 cup chopped bacon, ham or crabmeat

Blend all the ingredients except the cheese and bacon or whatever, and pour into pie pan. Sprinkle with the cheese and bacon etc, poking these under the surface, Cook 45 minutes or more if needed.

FRITTATA

Frittatas, sort of fried sandwiches, have always seemed to me rather daunting, but this one is very cooperative. It is best served with a fresh green salad at lunch.

> 3 yellow onions
> 1/3 cup olive oil
> 6 eggs
> 1/2 cup grated Parmigiano-Reggiano cheese

Peel and slice the onions and sauté them with the oil for 15 to 20 minutes over medium heat; do not let them brown.

Meanwhile whisk eggs until frothy, add the cheese and seasonings.

When the onions are soft, pour the eggs mixture over them, stirring to cover, and let them cook until brown on the bottom and set in the middle, about 12 minutes. Then flip it over and cook about two more minutes. Cut into wedges and serve with Our Special Salt.

Serves 4 or 5

IMITATION CHEESE SOUFFLE

8 slices white bread
1 pound sharp cheddar cheese, grated
4 eggs, beaten
2 cup milk
salt and pepper

Butter an 8-cup soufflé dish. Cut crusts off bread and butter each slice on one side and cut into four sections. Pile half the bread, buttered side, up, in the dish and cover with half the cheese, and then layer the rest of the bread and top with remaining cheese, mix the eggs and milk and pour into the dish. Cover and refrigerate overnight.

Heat oven to 350 degrees.

Uncover the soufflé and bake on center rack for about 45 minutes, until top is brown and there is bubbling at the edges. Serve as soon as possible!

ONION TART

Set oven at 350 degrees.

> **frozen pie crust**
> **3 cup sliced onions**
> **3 tablespoon butter**
> **Salt and pepper**
> **2 beaten eggs**
> **7/8 cup sour cream**
> **1/4 teaspoon nutmeg**
> **1/3 cup grated Gruyere cheese**

Bake piecrust according to directions on package. Sauté onions in butter, covered, about 20 minutes, until they are yellow and tender. Combine eggs, sour cream, and nutmeg.

Put onions in crust, cover with sour cream mix, and top with cheese.

Bake 30 minutes until set and lightly browned.

Serves 6-8

ONION AND TOMATO TART

Set oven to 350 degrees.

> **baked piecrust**
> **3 tablespoons butter**
> **3 large onions, sliced**
> **2 red tomatoes**
> **1 yellow tomato**
> **1/2 cup grated Gruyere cheese**

Sauté the onion slices in the butter, covered, for 15 or 20 minutes, then uncover and let them get nice and caramelized. Put them over the piecrust, then add the cheese.

Slice the tomatoes into thin slices, then quarter and arrange them, overlapping, on the outside of the crust. Continue in the second row, overlapping in a different direction. Fill in the center with the yellow slices.

Bake for an hour.

Serves 8

QUICHES

Quiches look (and sound) elegant, yet are incredibly simple to produce. They all need a baked pie shell. (And you know where to get those!) Many are made with cheese, usually Gruyere, sometimes Parmesan. Try Roquefort for a new flavor. Some quiches have only eggs and heavy cream instead of cheese. Feel free to be creative with your quiche; there are many things one might add: ham, bacon, mushrooms, crab, or lobster.

A small serving of quiche makes a very nice first course.

TRADITIONAL QUICHE LORRAINE

Set oven at 350 degrees.

>   **baked piecrust**
>   **1 pound lean bacon**
>   **2 tablespoons butter**
>   **2 cup heavy cream**
>   **1/2 teaspoon salt**
>   **1/4 teaspoon nutmeg**
>   **3 eggs, beaten**

Prepare piecrust according to package directions. Fry the bacon in the butter till crisp and set aside. Beat the eggs. Bring the cream, salt, and nutmeg to a boil and pour over the eggs, stirring constantly. Crumble the bacon over the piecrust, then add the egg mixture and bake 25 or 30 minute until set.

Serves 6-8

MUSHROOM/CHEESE QUICHE

Set oven to 350 degrees.

>   baked piecrust
>   1 1/2 tablespoon butter
>   1 cup sliced mushrooms
>   1/3 cup sliced scallions
>   1 1/2 tablespoons butter
>   2 tablespoons chopped parsley
>   salt and pepper
>   2 eggs
>   2 egg yolks
>   1/2 teaspoon nutmeg
>   1 cup heavy cream
>   1/2 cup shredded Gruyere

Prepare piecrust according to package directions. Heat half the butter till very hot and bubbly, so that when you add the mushrooms they will brown and not become weak and soggy. When done, fry the scallions separately in the rest of the butter for a few minutes. Sprinkle these ingredients onto the pie shell with the parsley and salt and pepper. Beat the eggs with the nutmeg. Scald the cream, and pour it over the eggs, stirring faithfully. Add mixture to the pie shell. Top with the Gruyere and bake 20 or 25 minutes.

Serves 6

EASIEST QUICHE

Heat oven to 350 degrees.

> 2 frozen pastry shells, defrosted
> 1 can French fried onions
> 4 eggs, beaten
> Our Special Salt and some pepper
> 1 large can evaporated milk
> 1 1/2 cup grated cheddar

Roll piecrusts together to make one large crust, put in 12-inch tart pan; make a rolled edge with overlapping dough. When cool, put onions in pie shells; add eggs, milk, and seasoning. Top with cheese. Bake for 20-25 minutes and serve in thin wedges.

Serves 8

SMORRBROD

Smorrbrod, which also is translated as "smorgasbord" is an assortment of small open sandwiches with various toppings. We had them in Copenhagen, where even restaurants in department stores have amazing choices of this local favorite.

The sandwiches always come on a half piece of bread—dark, white, or rye—with the crusts cut off. A raw egg yolk , nestled in an onion ring, often embellishes it. This may sound icky but it makes the whole thing nice and moist.

If you are going to serve a smorrbrod you should have an assortment of three or four choices, Here are some ideas, but make up your own personal smorrbord, too.

1.

cold pork slices
relish
mayonnaise

Arrange the pork on buttered bread spread with mayo, Add a dab of relish on top.

2.

radishes
butter
scallions
sliced black olives

Cut the radishes very thin and layer them on heavily-buttered bread. Decorate with the olives and top with a frizzle of scallions.

3.

Danish blue cheese
raw onion ring
raw egg yolk
bread and butter

Butter the bread, spread with cheese, add an onion ring with center removed to hold the egg yolk.

4.

cooked shrimp
lettuce leaf
mayonnaise
lemon slice

Cut the shrimp in half and remove the tails. Spread the bread with mayonnaise, top with a lettuce leaf cut to fit the bread, and add the shrimp.

You could also do a big platter and let the guests make their own sandwiches. Offer raw, sliced onion, sliced tomatoes, hardboiled eggs, liverwurst, herring and a variety of cheeses and some small shrimp.

Small diced potatoes are traditional, as are pickled beets and chopped dill pickles. Decorate the platter with parsley and lettuce and watch the guests have fun.

SPICY SAUSAGE CASEROLE

Ann Watson does it again!

Heat oven to 350 degrees.

> **1 pound spicy pork sausage (like Jimmy Dean's)**
> **3/4 cup Bisquick**
> **3/4 pound sharp Cheddar**

Mix ingredients in ovenproof dish and bake 20-25 minutes until brown.

Serves 6

Meat

$\mathcal{D}$uring our skiing days we used to put a leg of lamb in the oven in the morning at the lowest possible temperature and leave it there all day while we hit the slopes. Then, about half an hour before dinner, we set the oven up to 300 degrees and usually the lamb turned out tender and delicious. But I say "usually" because there were some failures, when the meat was too done or too rare. So this is not a guaranteed recipe, but worth a try, especially if you have an electric oven, which can be set lower than gas. Someone said this method was "like putting the lamb out on the sidewalk on a hot day."

Here's the normal way to roast a leg of lamb.

LEG OF LAMB

Heat oven to 450 degrees.

> **5 pound leg of lamb**
> **slivers of garlic**
> **rosemary**
> **mint sauce**

Stab the lamb with a pointed knife and insert slivers of garlic or rosemary.

Put the meat, fat side up, in a roasting pan. Reduce the oven heat to 350 degrees when you put the lamb in the oven. Cook 25 or 30 minutes to the pound...to an internal temperature of 160 degrees for rare and 180 degrees for well done.

If you want gravy, remove the meat from the pan and keep about 3 tablespoons pan drippings, add 3 tablespoon flour and mix well. Use a cup of water sour cream or stock, add slowly, stirring constantly. Season to taste.

Lamb is usually served with mint jelly or mint sauce.

MEAT LOAF

A good meatloaf can almost be improvised. They all require ground beef and pork sausage. Sometimes ground ham is added. Then there are eggs, ketchup, and sometimes minced onions. You might like lot of sautéed chopped vegetables or fresh herbs.

When my children were young I had concocted a meat loaf for them and was going to add a mushroom sauce for their father and me. I asked our baby sitter to slice the mushrooms. She did, her way; she sliced the stems and threw the caps down the disposal.

Here's a basic meatloaf recipe.

Heat oven to 350 degrees.

> 2 pounds ground beef
> 1 pound ground pork or pork sausage (Jimmy Dean's)
> 1 onion finely chopped
> 3 tablespoons olive oil
> 2 eggs, beaten
> 1/4 cup milk
> 3/4 cup plain or seasoned breadcrumbs
> 3/4 cup ketchup
> Our Special Salt and pepper

Sauté onions in the olive oil.

Mix the meat, pulling at it with two forks; you may have to use your hands. Then add the eggs, the breadcrumbs, ketchup, and the milk. Add the cooled onions, Our Special Salt and pepper. Form it into a loaf and place in a baking pan or casserole and bake for an hour, maybe more, until nicely firm. Let the meatloaf stand for five or ten minutes before slicing it into rather thick portions.

Very good for sandwiches the next day!

Serves 8

PARTY HAMBURGERS

This Scandinavian open-face sandwich is an interesting surprise for an informal dinner party.

> 8 slices rye bread
> 2 pounds ground round steak
> 1 cup chopped capers, drained
> 1/4 teaspoon allspice
> 2 egg yolks
> 2 teaspoons salt
> 3/4 teaspoons pepper
> 8 ounce can beets, chopped (save the juice)
> 1/4 cup beet juice
> 1/4 cup heavy cream

Toast the bread lightly.

Mix the meat, capers, allspice, egg yolks and salt and pepper in a bowl. Mix the juice, cream, and beets in large measuring cup. Add this to the meat mixture. Spread the hamburgers thickly on the toast and broil about 7 inches from the heat for 5 minutes or more, depending on how well done you like the meat.

Serve with rice and green beans.

Serves 8

PORK CHOPS, TENDER

Allow four hours for these strangely adorned chops to bake. Henry VIII, with his enormous appetite, would have been a happy guest.

Heat oven to 200 degrees.

> **6 2-inch thick pork chops; double ones, really**
> **ketchup**
> **1 onion**
> **brown sugar**
> **lemon slice for each chop**

Spread ketchup on each chop, add a thick slice of onion, and then a layer of brown sugar. Place a rather thick slice of lemon on top of each chop and bake 4 hours. They will be surprisingly tender and flavorful!

Serves 6.

PORK CHOPS IN SOUR CREAM

Heat oven to 350 degrees.

6 pork chops, with or without the bone
seasoned flour
2 tablespoons vinegar
2 tablespoons sugar
1 cup sour cream
2 bay leaves

Dip chops in flour and shake off excess; place in ovenproof dish. Mix vinegar, sugar, sour cream and pour over meat, add a few bay leaves. Bake an hour.

Serves 4-6

PORK TENDERLOIN

There are dozens of no-muss no-fuss ways to prepare pork tenderloin, and it is a fairly economical party dish. I get the packaged kind in the "pork" section.

My favorite way to cook one is a bit messy but awfully good.

PORK TENDERLOIN WITH HONEY SESAME

Heat over to 400 degrees.

> **1 packaged two-pound pork tenderloin**
> **1 cup soy sauce**
> **3 cloves garlic, minced**
> **2 tablespoons minced fresh ginger**
> **2 tablespoons sesame oil**
> **1/2 cup honey**
> **4 tablespoons brown sugar**
> **5 tablespoons black sesame seeds**

Combine soy sauce, garlic, ginger and sesame oil. Pour this over the tenderloin, spreading evenly, and let marinate two hours at room temperature or overnight in the refrigerator.

When ready to cook, remove pork from marinade. Mix together honey and brown sugar (this is where the messiness begins) and roll pork in this mixture. Then sprinkle with sesame seeds; if you have no black seeds, use white ones.

Roast pork in a shallow pan for 20-30 minutes, until meat thermometer registers 155 degrees.

Carve in very thin slices.

Serves 8

ROAST BONE MARROW WITH PARSLEY SALAD

I had been buying marrow bones for my dog until I went to London and had roast bone marrow with parsley on toast at Fergus Henderson's award-winning restaurant, St. John. It was delicious!

And, I'm sorry to say, much too good even for my special doggie.

You will need ice tea spoons or something similar to remove the marrow.

Fergus has been named best chef in England this year (2004), and St. John was recently voted one of the 50 best restaurants in the world! (It was sixteenth.)

Here is a typical recipe from his new American cookbook, *The Whole Beast* ("Nose to Tail Eating"), an amusing as well as an informative guide to unusual dishes.

Along with recipes he also gives advice. I particularly liked this bit: "Do not be afraid of cooking as your ingredients will know and misbehave."

> 12 3-inch pieces of veal marrow bone
> a healthy bunch of flat leaf parsley leaves, picked from the stem
> 2 shallots, peeled and very thinly sliced
> 1 modest handful capers, extra fine if possible

DRESSING

> juice of one lemon
> extra-virgin olive oil
> pinch of sea salt and freshly ground black pepper
> a good supply of toast
> coarse sea salt

Put the marrowbone pieces in an ovenproof frying pan and into a hot oven 450. The roasting process should take about 20 minutes depending on the thickness of the bone. You are looking for the marrow to be loose and giving, but not melted away, which it will do if left too long. (Traditionally the ends would be covered to prevent any seepage but I like the coloring and crispness at the ends.)

Meanwhile, lightly chop your parsley, just enough to discipline it, mix it with the shallots and capers, and at the last moment, dress the salad.

Here is a dish that should be completely seasoned before leaving the kitchen, rendering a last-minute seasoning unnecessary by the actual eater; this, especially in the case of the coarse sea salt, gives texture and uplift to the moment of eating. My approach is to scrape the marrow from the bone onto the toast and season it with coarse sea salt. Then a pinch of parsley salad on top of this and eat. Of course once you have your pile of marrow, salad, toast and salt it is the diner's choice.

A note from Fergus adds: Do you remember eating Raisin Bran for breakfast? The raisin-to-bran-flake ratio was always a huge anxiety, to a point, sometimes, that one was tempted to add extra raisins, which inevitably resulted in too many raisins, and one lost that pleasure of discovering the occasional sweet chewiness in contrast to the branny crunch. When administering such things as capers, it is very good to remember Raisin Bran.

Poultry

BALSAMIC VINEGAR CHICKEN

This is laughably simple and has a wonderful flavor. If you feel extravagant, use more shallots. I had it first in Santa Fe at Carla and Bruce Friedlich's. The chicken cooked; we played bridge.

Heat oven to 350 degrees.

> **chicken thighs (allow 2 per person)**
> **shallots**
> **good balsamic vinegar**

Peel and quarter the shallots, put them in a large baking dish with the chicken. Cover the chicken halfway with vinegar, cover pan with foil, and bake half an hour. Remove foil and bake another half hour. Good with noodles or rice.

BASIC ROAST CHICKEN

Set oven to 400 degrees.

> **chicken**
> **rosemary sprigs (optional)**
> **2 whole lemons**
> **Our Special Salt**

Allow one pound of neat per person. Remove neck, giblets and liver from the chicken and wash inside with cold water, then dry thoroughly. Put the lemons in the cavity for flavor, with a few rosemary sprigs. Loosen the breast and thigh skin with your finger, and tuck the rosemary and some of Our Special Salt under the skin before baking.

Cook on a rack in a small heavy casserole covered, for fifteen minutes. Then turn oven down to 350 degrees and bake another 45 minutes.

CHINESE CHICKEN AND WALNUTS

When served with rice, this is perfect for a large party. It does have more than our usual paltry number of ingredients, but it is still quite simple to prepare.

> 1 1/2 cups walnuts
> 3 cups boned chicken breasts, cut into slivers
> 5 tablespoons butter
> 1 cup sliced water chestnuts
> 1 cup diced celery
> 12 diced scallions
> 2 boxes frozen French cut green beans
> 2 garlic cloves, diced
> 3 tablespoons minced fresh ginger
> 3 cups chicken broth
> 2 1/2 teaspoons salt
> 1 teaspoon pepper
> 1 tablespoon sugar
> 3 tablespoons corn starch

Sauté walnuts in one-tablespoon butter over low heat; drain on paper towels.

Sauté chicken in 4 tablespoons butter until meat turns white, add chestnuts, celery, scallions, beans, garlic, and ginger. Simmer briefly, add broth, soy sauce, sugar and seasonings and simmer till beans are done, Mix the cornstarch with a little of the liquid and add it to chicken mixture; then add the rest, stirring as it thickens.

Sprinkle the dish with walnuts and serve.

Serves 8-10

HERBED CHICKEN BREASTS

This has a very nice flavor not often found in a chicken dish and is a good dinner-party dish.

Set oven to 300 degrees.

> 4 slices diced bacon
> 2 tablespoons butter
> 6 boned chicken breasts, cut in half
> 2 teaspoons salt
> 1 teaspoons allspice
> 1 teaspoon cinnamon
> 3 minced scallions
> 3 tablespoons chopped parsley
> 2/3 cup white wine
> 2/3 cup chicken broth
> 2 slightly beaten egg yolks

Sauté bacon in the butter till crispy; remove. Mix the salt, allspice, and cinnamon and sprinkle the mixture on the chicken then sauté in the remaining butter about ten minutes until meat turns white. Transfer chicken to a baking dish and put in oven for 10-15 minutes while preparing sauce.

Make sauce by adding scallions and parsley to hot fat in skillet, sauté for a few minutes, then add the wine and broth; heat and reduce for about five minutes. Beat a small amount of broth into the egg yolks, stirring, and then gradually add all the liquid to the eggs. Pour over chicken and serve with rice and green peas.

Serves 8

CHINESE LEMON CHICKEN

"Pearl's" was a popular New York restaurant in the 1960s , particularly with Time/Life people, many of whom had invested in the restaurant when Pearl started it. This is an adaptation of her famous lemon chicken.

Our advice is to limit your guests to four or six when making this dish; it is rather hectic to prepare more.

> chicken breasts, boned and skinned
> 2 tablespoons soy sauce
> 1/4 teaspoon sesame oil
> 1 tablespoon gin or vodka
> 3 egg whites, beaten until frothy
> 1 cup water chestnut flour (available at Oriental shops)
> 1/2 cup peanut oil
> iceberg lettuce, sliced

LEMON SAUCE

> 3/4 cup sugar
> 1/2 cup white vinegar
> 1 cup chicken broth
> 3 tablespoons cornstarch
> 2 tablespoons water
> I lemon, juice and chopped zest
> 1/3 of 1 ounce bottle lemon extract

Slice the chicken breasts into 1 inch wide long slices. Mix soy sauce, sesame oil, and gin or vodka and marinate chicken slices in this for an hour.

Make the sauce, mixing the sugar, vinegar, broth, and lemon juice and zest. When it is simmering, add the water to the cornstarch, stir, add a bit of the sauce, stir and then add to simmering mixture.

Dip the marinated slices into the egg whites and then into water chestnut powder. (This gives the chicken an amazing extra crunchiness but regular flour or rice flour could be used).

Sauté the chicken in peanut oil in a heavy skillet until light brown and crisp. Make individual portions of lettuce slices; divide the chicken onto the lettuce.

Add the lemon extract to the sauce at the last minute and pour over the chicken and lettuce.

Serve with simple white rice with plenty of butter.

Fish

*A*n easy and foolproof way to cook fish is to bake it in hot butter, sort of a bake/fry method.

Heat oven to 350 degrees.

> **perch, trout, or any white fish**
> **flour**
> **1 stick of butter**
> **fresh herbs**
> **parsley**
> **1 lemon**

Dip the fish in flour. For four servings, put a stick of butter in a glass baking dish and put into the oven. When the butter is bubbling and beginning to brown, slide the fish into the pan and cook for about five minutes, basting one or two times. Add herbs, a few squeezes of lemon and parsley.

Serves 4

SALMON

Salmon lends itself to dozens of complements, marinades and spices; here are some suggestions for quick and satisfactory ways to prepare it.

WINE BAKED SALMON

Heat oven to 400 degrees.

> **2 pound salmon fillet**
> **1 cup water**
> **1 cup white wine**
> **salt and pepper**

Run your hand over the salmon to feel any little bones; these may be removed with needle-nose pliers.

Bring the water and wine to a boil and pour over salmon in a buttered baking dish, add salt and pepper. Cover with foil and bake in middle of oven for 20 or 25 minutes.

Serves 6

GAIL'S MARINATED SALMON

Gail Zweigenthal, former editor of Gourmet magazine, fixed this salmon for dinner at Chris Haynes and Jeff Harakal's, my-next-door-neighbors, in Santa Fe. Of course, it was delicious. And easy, too.

When ready to cook, heat broiler.

> **2 pound salmon fillet**
> **1/3 cup sesame seeds**
> **1 cup sherry**
> **1/3 cup soy sauce**
> **1/4 teaspoon minced fresh ginger**
> **1/3 cupsesame oil**
> **1/3/4 cups scallions, thinly sliced**
> **2 tablespoons minced garlic**

Mix sesame seeds, sherry, soy sauce, ginger, sesame oil, scallions, and garlic. Marinate salmon in this mixture at room temperature for an hour or more. Cook the salmon in the broiler four inches under the flame for about twelve minutes.

Serves 8

SALMON WITH ANCHOVY SAUCE
(baked or broiled)

> salmon fillet
> 1/4 cup sour cream
> 1 teaspoon anchovy paste (or more)
> 1 1/2/ tablespoons lemon zest
> 11/2 tablespoons minced parsley
> 2 garlic cloves, pressed

Mix the ingredients and spread in a thin layer on fish before cooking.

You may bake the salmon at 375 degrees for about 15 minutes or broil it for about ten or twelve minutes.

Serves 6

SCALLOPS WITH HOLLANDAISE

This is a nice, simple, reliable way to prepare scallops.

Heat oven to 375 degrees.

> **1 pound scallops**
> **1/2 cup seasoned bread crumbs**
> **1 tablespoon lemon juice**
> **1/4 cup wine or dry vermouth**
> **1 tablespoon chopped parsley**

Mix the breadcrumbs, lemon juice, vermouth and parsley and pour over the scallops in a baking dish. Bake for 15 minutes until bubbly.

HOLLANDAISE

> **3 egg yolks**
> **2 tablespoons lemon juice**
> **1/4 pound melted butter**
> **dash of salt**

Put egg yolks. lemon juice and salt into blender and pulse until mixed. Heat butter till boiling, being careful not to let it burn. Pour it very slowly into blender turned to high speed. Continue blending only about 30 seconds, until sauce is thick. You may keep it warm in a double boiler over warm water if you do not use it at once.

Serves 4

SAUTEED SCALLOPS

1 pound scallops
juice of two lemons
3 tablespoons parsley
4 tablespoons butter

Fry the scallops in two tablespoons butter till lightly brown.
Cut them in half. Roll the lemon and squeeze the juice over
the scallops; add parsley and tarragon to pan; work in two
tablespoons of butter. Do not let this boil.

Vegetables

$\mathcal{F}$resh vegetables are so good with only butter and fresh chopped herbs like basil, tarragon, chives or parsley, that they needn't be all gussied up. But some of these recipes offer new tastes and flavors you might like to try.

Asparagus looks very elegant peeled....but should we even mention this in a hardly-any-cooking book? If you are going to peel it, start about two inches from the tops, and you might as well cut the stalks neatly, the same length, instead of snapping them off.

ASPARAGUS WITH BLACK SESAME SEED

2 pounds asparagus, trimmed
3 tablespoons melted butter
3 tablespoons black sesame seeds

Steam until tender but still crisp. Transfer to platter, pour melted butter over it and sprinkle with sesame seeds.

If you cannot find black sesame seeds, try breadcrumbs sautéed in butter or crushed garlic in olive oil with Parmesan cheese as a topping. This last one you can run under the broiler for a minute or so till it browns a little.

Serves 8

ASPARAGUS WITH GARLIC

Heat oven to 350 degrees.

> **2 pounds asparagus, trimmed**
> **3/4 cup vegetable stock**
> **3 garlic cloves, chopped**
> **4 tablespoons olive oil**
> **1 lemon**
> **Our Special Salt and pepper**

Place asparagus neatly in a casserole, pour the vegetable stock over it, and then add olive oil, garlic, salt and pepper. Squeeze the lemon juice over all and bake 20-30 minutes until tender. Add Our Special Salt and pepper.

BEETS WITH SOUR CREAM

My favorite way to serve beets is this do-nothing treat.

> **1 can of chilled beets (for 2 or 3)**
> **sour cream**

Open the can. Drain the beets. Halve them if they seem too large. Serve them with in bowls with a big spoonful of sour cream on top of each.

BEET SOUFFLÉ

Set oven to 350 degrees.

> 8 cooked beets, diced
> juice of one lemon
> 2 tablespoons grated onions
> 4 egg yolks, beaten
> 1/4 cup cornstarch
> 5 egg whites, beaten

Beat the egg whites with a clean beater and set aside.

Put the beets, lemon juice and onions in a blender and puree.

Beat the egg yolks with the cornstarch and blend with the beet puree. Stir one-fourth of the egg whites into the puree, and then lightly fold in the rest.

Bake in a buttered 8-inch soufflé dish for 30 minutes.

STEAMED BEETS WITH TARRAGON

        1 bunch of beets
        2 tablespoons chopped tarragon
        1 tablespoon butter
        2 tablespoons chopped scallions
        1 teaspoon balsamic vinegar
        1/4 teaspoon sugar

Boil the beets and skin them while they are hot. Slice them crosswise 1/4 inch thick, toss them with the remaining ingredients; add salt and pepper to taste.

BROCCOLI

> 1 bunch broccoli
> salt and pepper
> 4 tablespoons melted butter
> breadcrumbs
> 1 tablespoon finely chopped scallions
> Parmesan cheese (optional)

Wash the broccoli and divide the florets into medium size portions. Cut the stalks into 1-inch lengths. Steam for about 10 minutes.

Melt 1 tablespoon butter and sauté the breadcrumbs and scallions in it briefly.

Serve the broccoli with 3 tablespoons butter and top it with the breadcrumb mix.

BRUSSELS SPROUTS

Brussels sprouts are very good served with butter and a little chopped parsley or chives.

> **1 pound Brussels sprouts**
> **2 tablespoons butter**
> **Our Special Salt**

Trim the bottoms of the sprouts and slice a deep "X" in the stem. Soak the sprouts in cold water for ten minutes and steam for about 12 minutes or boil for 10 minutes, until tender but firm.

Toss them 'round in the butter and salt and pepper them.

Serves 2 or 3

CAULIFLOWER WITH RICOTTA CHEESE

Heat oven to 375 degrees.

> **florets of a medium cauliflower**
> **2 tablespoons olive oil**
> **1/2 cup minced scallions**
> **3 tablespoons chopped chives**
> **1/4 cup chopped parsley**
> **1 cup ricotta cheese**
> **I egg white**
> **1/4 cup Parmesan cheese**
> **2 tablespoons breadcrumbs**

Steam cauliflower until tender but still crisp, drain and put in bowl. Drizzle florets with olive oil, then add scallions, chives, and parsley and toss gently. Put in a greased 8 by 11 inch baking dish.

Combine the ricotta with egg white and spoon over cauliflower in dollops. Combine Parmesan with breadcrumbs and add to topping.

Bake about 15 minutes, until hot and slightly brown.

Serves 6

CAULIFLOWER WITH PARMESAN

How would we dress up vegetables without the help of this staunch ally…Parmesan? If you are sick of this cheese, try plenty of buttered crumbs instead.

> 1 large cauliflower
> 3 cloves garlic, sliced thin
> 1/4 cup olive oil
> 2 tablespoons butter
> 1/2 cup Parmesan

Steam the cauliflower florets. While they are cooking, sauté the garlic in the olive oil and butter until it colors a little. Pour this over the cauliflower when it is done, and top with the cheese.

CARROTS JULIENNE

> 10 or 12 carrots
> 4 tablespoons butter
> 1 tablespoon brown sugar
> 1 teaspoon rice vinegar
> 1/4 cup chopped ginger
> 2 tablespoons chopped parsley

Scrub the carrots, cut off the ends and slice into long thin julienne sticks about a fourth of an inch wide. (Or cut into very thin slices on the diagonal.)

Steam carrots for fifteen minutes or boil them about twenty-five minutes.

In a saucepan melt the butter, and add the sugar, vinegar and ginger. Toss the carrots in this mix and add the parsley.

Serves 4

CARROTS AND PEANUTS

This is a great success with children who are not crazy about carrots.

> 8 medium carrots
> 2 tablespoons butter
> 3 tablespoons dry roasted peanuts, chopped
> 2 teaspoons honey
> 2 teaspoons lemon juice

Peel the carrots and slice them into diagonal half inch slices. Steam then for about fifteen minutes.

Melt the butter in a skillet and add the peanuts, then the honey and lemon juice; stir for a few minutes. Add this to the carrots and serve.

Serves 6

MASHED CARROTS

     2 bunches small carrots
     1/3 cup orange juice
     1 tablespoon orange zest
     1 tablespoon lemon juice
     1 tablespoon grated onion
     2 tablespoons butter
     1/4 cup melted butter
     1/4 teaspoon nutmeg or grated ginger root

Trim, scrub and mince the carrots. Cook them in a heavy pot, covered, with the juices, zest, onion and two tablespoons of butter. When they are tender, mash them with a potato masher or a fork and add the rest of the butter and the nutmeg.

Serves 4

CARROTS WITH ONIONS AND CREAM

2 cups chopped carrots
2 onion, sliced into 1 inch pieces
1 cup water
1 teaspoon sugar
3 tablespoons butter
2 tablespoons heavy cream
1/4 teaspoon ground cumin
salt and pepper to taste

Combine the carrots, onions, water, sugar, and one tablespoon of butter in a saucepan. Boil about 25 minutes, stirring occasionally, until the water has evaporated and the vegetables are beginning to brown. Off heat, stir in the remaining butter, cumin, cream and salt and pepper.

Serves 4

CORN

Fat Month

Fresh corn on the cob from a farmers' market or a nearby farm is the highlight of summer eating! We used to call August "fat month" because of the all the fresh corn we consumed.

It needs very little boiling; do not overcook it. If there are any leftover ears, slice down the rows of kernels with a sharp knife and then press the rows down with the side of a fork, scraping out the milk and heart and leaving the skin on the cob. Now you have the best of the corn to warm up with butter. Yum yum.

CORN ON THE COB

fresh corn
boiling water or mixed milk and water
butter
salt
freshly ground pepper

Remove the husks and silk from freshly picked corn.

Drop the corn ear by ear into the water, being careful not to stop the boiling. After about four minutes, pick the ears out of the water in the order they were dropped in.

You know what to do with butter and salt! Provide plenty of napkins; paper ones are almost necessary with corn on the cob.

CORN PUDDING

Set oven to 350 degrees.

> **2/3 cup flour**
> **3 eggs, beaten**
> **2 tablespoons butter, melted**
> **1 cup heavy cream**
> **1 teaspoon salt**
> **2 tablespoons sugar**
> **1 cup corn, canned, frozen or fresh**

Mix flour with eggs to a smooth paste, add butter, cream, salt, and sugar. Beat vigorously, and then add corn. Let stand an hour or so, then pour into a buttered baking dish; set it in a pan of hot water and bake 30 or 40 minutes. A knife should come out clean, although it's okay if the middle is a little runny.

Serves 4

EGGPLANT

A Sometimes Recalcitrant Vegetable

Here is a very successful way of cooking this sometimes recalcitrant vegetable.

> **whole eggplant, peeled**
> **salt**
> **flour**
> **4 tablespoons olive oil**

Slice eggplant rather thinly and salt both sides of each slice. Put in a colander for an hour or two. (Put it in the sink or over a bowl; it "weeps.") Rinse off the salt and flour the slices, or leave them bare.

Sauté in the olive oil over high heat until brown and crisp. If you have a grill pan, it makes nice ridges on eggplant fried this way.

Serves 4

DEEP FRIED EGGPLANT

>2 eggplants
>2 eggs, slightly beaten
>3 tablespoons water
>3 tablespoons grated Parmesan cheese
>3/4 cup flour
>2 cups fine breadcrumbs
>6 cups corn or vegetable oil

Peel and slice eggplant about 3/4 of an inch thick; salt the slices and let them "weep" in a colander for an hour or two.

Cut the slices into sticks, as wide as they are thick.

Mix the egg with the water, Parmesan, and salt and pepper and beat.

Dip the eggplant sticks in flour to coat well, and then in egg mixture, again coating well. Coat the slices uniformly in breadcrumbs and transfer to a flat dish.

Heat the oil in a deep fryer or heavy pan to 375 degrees (or until a drop of water put into it sputters instantly.) Add the eggplant, a big handful at a time and cook for three minutes. Remove slices with slotted spoon, let drain and put on paper towels. Repeat.

Serves 6

GREEN BEANS

A childhood treat for me was green beans with sliced toasted almonds! It may be old-fashioned, but it's still my favorite way to serve this vegetable.

Green beans are very obliging and useful, and happily, available all year long. Here are some other ways to jazz up beans for company. Frozen ones may be substituted in most of these recipes.

GREEN BEANS AND WATER CHESTNUTS

> 3 tablespoons olive oil
> 11/2-pound green beans, ends trimmed or 3
>   boxes frozen green beans
> 1 can sliced water chestnuts
> 1 tablespoon sugar
> 1 teaspoon salt
> 1 teaspoon cornstarch
> 1/4 cup chicken stock

Stir-fry beans a few minutes in the olive oil; add salt, sugar, water chestnuts, and stir. Add the chicken stock and cook until beans are tender but crisp; about ten minutes.

Put the cornstarch in a few tablespoons of the liquid and mix well. Then put this back into the bean mix, stirring. When it begins to thicken it is ready to serve.

Serves 6

BEAN MEDLEY

> 4 tablespoons chopped walnuts
> 1 pound green beans, trimmed
> 1 pound wax beans, trimmed
> 1 1/2 tablespoons butter
> 2 tablespoons olive oil
> 1 clove garlic, minced
> 2 tablespoons minced parsley
> 2 tablespoons lemon juice

Sauté walnuts in oil and butter; set aside.

Trim ends of beans and slice diagonally into two inch pieces. Cook them in a large pot of boiling water about ten minutes until tender but crisp. Drain and add garlic, parsley and lemon juice; garnish with walnuts.

Serves 8

GREEN BEANS AND MUSHROOMS

This nice party dish is a little different.

> **2 pounds green beans**
> **2 tablespoons butter**
> **1 cup sliced mushrooms**
> **2/3 cup sour cream**
> **2 tablespoons chopped parsley**

Snip off the ends of the beans, sliver them, slice them on the diagonal or leave them whole.

Cook them for about 20 minutes in boiling water to which you have added a little lemon juice or vinegar to preserve the color.

While the beans are cooking, sauté the sliced mushrooms in butter, mix in the parsley and sour cream.

Garnish the drained beans with the mushroom mix and serve.

Serves 8

MUSHROOMS

Even though mushrooms grow in the dark, they are bursting with vitamin D, the sunshine vitamin. They add a bit of zip to rice as well as to many vegetable dishes.

When sautéing mushrooms have the butter or oil nice and hot before you add the mushrooms, lest they get limp and soggy.

STUFFED PORTABELLO OR WHITE MUSHROOMS

1 onion, finely chopped
2 minced garlic cloves
3 tablespoons olive oil
I tablespoon butter
4 portabello or 12 large white mushrooms
1/4 cup white wine
1/2 cup chopped parsley or chives,

Sauté the bread crumbs in the butter until lightly brown and set aside.

Chop the mushroom stems and sauté them with the onion and garlic in two tablespoons of oil for about three minutes. Add half the breadcrumbs and one fourth cup of wine to this mixture. Set aside.

In a pan large enough for all the mushrooms to be turned gill-sides down, heat the rest of the oil and add the mushrooms, Cook about five minutes. They will exude juices. Turn them over and cook for a few more minutes. Add the juices to breadcrumb mixture and fill the mushrooms.

Serve as a side dish sprinkled with parsley or chives.

Serves 6

ONIONS

Onions are a wonderful accompaniment to almost any dish...simply sautéed until caramelized, creamed, seasoned, or baked in a tart. Here are two tarts, one to be baked with uncooked onions that comes out crisp and oniony, the other with cooked onions, that yields a smoother and richer dish. Try them both.

ONION TART I

Heat oven to 400 degrees.

> **pastry shell**
> **3 large onions**
> **3 tablespoons Dijon mustard**
> **11/2 tablespoons olive oil**
> **salt and pepper**

Slice the onions, toss in a bowl with the mustard and olive oil. Pile in an unbaked pastry shell; bake 20 minutes till onions have browned slightly.

Serves 6

ONION TART II

Heat oven to 450 degrees.

> **pastry shell**
> **4 onions, sliced**
> **6 tablespoons butter**
> **2 egg yolks**
> **2 tablespoons heavy cream**
> **salt and lots of pepper**
> **teaspoon grated nutmeg**

Cook the onions gently in butter for 30 or 40 minutes, covered. Raise lid and cook 5 minutes more to caramelize onions. Put them in the pastry shell.

Mix egg yolks, cream, salt and pepper, and nutmeg. Pour into pastry shell on top of the onions and bake 20 minutes.

Serves 8

ROAST STUFFED ONIONS

Heat oven to 375 degrees.

> 6 large red onions or Spanish onions
> 2 cups cooked rice
> 3 cloves crushed garlic
> 1/2 cup chopped walnuts
> 2 cups grated Monterey Jack cheese
> 3/4 cup red wine

Hollow out the onions with a knife and spoon before you roast them for 20 minutes,

Mix rice, garlic, walnuts and cheese, and stuff the onions with the mixture when they are done. Put in a baking dish, pour the wine over the onions and bake 30 minutes more.

Serves 6

OMAHA ONION RINGS

My father's deep fried onions were SENSATIONAL! He was very particular about his recipe, and insisted that once sliced, the onions must be soaked overnight in milk.

He also gave me dire warnings about deep-frying. An electric fryer is not vital, but a frying thermometer is. A heavy kettle or saucepan with a flat bottom will serve. Never fill it more than halfway with oil. Heat the oil slowly so any moisture will evaporate. Do not allow the fat to smoke. Do not try to fry too many onions at a time. Try to have them at room temperature.

A wire basket is useful; a slotted spoon and a lot of paper towels are necessary.

No need to be cowardly…go for it.

OMAHA ONION RINGS

>   5 large white onions
>   2 quarts milk
>   2 cups flour
>   vegetable oil
>   salt and pepper

Peel and thinly slice the onions. Separate them into rings.
Soak them overnight in the refrigerator in a large bowl filled
with milk.

When ready to fry, drain the onions, and then shake them
in a paper bag with flour. Heat the oil and when you think
it is 350-375 degrees, take its temperature. (If you don't have
a thermometer, test fry a small cube of bread: if it toasts in
one minute, the oil is at about 375).

Lower about a handful of onions at a time into the fat and
brown them lightly. Remove them to paper towels, drain,
and salt them.

Serves 4-5

PARSNIPS

The Poor Pitiful Parsnip

The poor, pitiful, parsnip! Largely scorned and ignored, it deserves a better fate. One cook, Stella Standard, was very pro-parsnip; the following recipe is adapted from her book, Cook Book.

London chef Fergus Henderson (who gave us the recipe for roast marrowbone) is another fan of parsnips. He cooks his in milk until they are tender and then mashes them with butter.

Many cookbooks especially fancy ones, have not a single recipe for the humble parsnip!

PARSNIPS WITH ORANGE

Heat oven to 500 degrees.

> **2 pounds young parsnips, peeled**
> **1 tablespoon olive oil**
> **1 teaspoon salt**
> **1/2 teaspoon freshly ground pepper**
> **grated zest of a large orange**
> **juice of one orange**

Trim the ends and cut the parsnips into large matchsticks, removing any woody core. Put them in a bowl with the olive oil and salt and pepper; toss to coat. Turn them into a large roasting pan and roast in oven, shaking occasionally. Roast until they have caramelized, about 5 to 10 minutes. Transfer to warm bowl and serve.

Serves 8

BAKED PARSNIPS

Heat oven to 375 degrees.

> **4 parsnips (one pound)**
> **3 tablespoons butter**
> **salt and pepper**
> **1/2 cup brown sugar**
> **1/2 cup vegetable or chicken stock**

Pare the parsnips and cut them into quarters. Put butter in a baking dish, add the parsnips, turning them to get them nicely coated. Add salt and sprinkle with brown sugar. Pour stock into dish and bake for 45 minutes.

Serves 4

PEAS

It is actually possible to put a package of room-temperature, defrosted frozen peas into a food processor, whirr them for a few seconds, and have them taste like fresh peas. It's amazing.

Fresh peas do not need to boil away madly for a long time, and frozen ones need hardly any boiling at all.

PEAS WITH MINT AND GREEN ONIONS

> **2 pounds fresh peas or two packages frozen peas**
> **4 or five green onions**
> **1 tablespoon mint, coarsely chopped**
> **4 tablespoons butter**
> **salt and pepper**

Slice the green onions and sauté them with the butter and salt and pepper until they are a little tender.

Put fresh peas in a pot with the onions and four tablespoons water, cover tightly and cook 10 or 12 minutes. You may add a little more butter if they seem to need it when they are done.

For frozen peas, boil a small amount of water, when it is boiling add the peas and let them simmer for about four minutes. Drain them and add the onions, butter, salt and pepper and the mint.

DAUPHINOIS POTATOES GRATIN

When you see that French word "Dauphinois" think "rich." It means heavy cream, lots of cheese, eggs and milk. But the good news: hardly any of the now dreaded "carbs."

Heat oven to 375 degrees.

> **3 pounds potatoes (Yukon gold or Idaho russet)**
> **3 cups milk (or half and half if you are feeling thin)**
> **1 cup heavy cream**
> **1 garlic clove**
> **1 cup grated Gruyere**
> **3 tablespoons butter**

Peel and slice the potatoes thinly. Bring the milk to a boil and add the potatoes; cook until they are done but not mushy. Rub the inside of a baking dish with the garlic, add the potatoes, add the heavy cream, and top with the cheese. Cut the butter into little bits and strew it around the top.

Bake for 15 minutes until the top is golden.

Serves 8

SLICED BAKED POTATOES

Heat oven to 350 degrees.

> **6 large baking potatoes**
> **8 tablespoons butter**
> **3 tablespoons minced parsley**
> **Our Special Salt and pepper**

Prick the potatoes with a fork and bake for an hour, or until done.

Melt the butter and stir in the parsley.

Cut the potatoes crosswise into slices 1/3 inch thick with the skins, arrange them, overlapping, on a serving platter. Drizzle the parsley butter over all and add salt and pepper.

Serves 6 or 8

SPINACH

I don't know why spinach isn't at every party, it is so good, and full of iron and magnesium and other admirable things, Maybe it's shunned because it turns guests' teeth green? Or perhaps hostesses have found that what was meant to feed eight has shrunk to three measly portions.

SPINACH WITH PINE NUTS

> 3 boxes frozen chopped spinach (or 3 pounds
>   fresh, if you insist)
> 2 garlic cloves, peeled and coarsely chopped
> 3 tablespoons olive oil
> 1/2 cup pine nuts
> salt and pepper

Cook the spinach according to package directions, drain well, pushing it into (not through) a strainer.

Heat the oil in a medium size skillet, add the garlic and cook it a minute or two. Don't let it brown. Discard the garlic. Sauté the pine nuts in the oil one or two minutes, add the spinach and stir gently three or four minutes.

Serves 6

SPINACH CASSEROLE

This is a little simpler than a spinach soufflé and it puffs up, too.

Heat oven to 400 degrees.

> 3 boxes frozen chopped spinach
> 2 tablespoons olive oil
> 2 chopped onions
> 6 eggs
> 1 teaspoon grated nutmeg
> 1 3/4 grated Cheddar cheese
> 1/4 teaspoon cayenne
> salt and pepper

Cook and drain the spinach. Put in medium bowl. Sauté the onions in olive oil about 5 minutes, add to spinach. In separate bowl, beat eggs with nutmeg, add to spinach and stir. Put spinach mix in a shallow buttered casserole. Mix cheese and cayenne, sprinkle on top of spinach in casserole. Bake 35 minutes until spinach is puffed and cheese is brown.

Serves 6

SPINACH WITH SOUR CREAM

> 3 boxes frozen chopped spinach
> 1 tablespoon butter
> 1/2 cup sour cream
> 1/8 teaspoon grated nutmeg
> salt and pepper

Cook the spinach as usual; drain it well. Dress it with butter, nutmeg, salt and pepper. Top it with sour cream.

Serves 6 (meagerly)

TURNIPS

Turnips are almost as misunderstood as parsnips; I hated them as a child, but now find mashed or pureed turnips rather soothing and a good excuse to use a lot of butter.

MASHED TURNIPS

> 2 pounds turnips
> 3 tablespoons orange juice
> zest from one orange
> 4 tablespoons butter
> 1/2 teaspoon nutmeg

Quarter the turnips and put them in a large pot of cold water, bring to a boil. Cook until tender, about 15-20 minutes.

Drain them well and puree in a food processor (or mash). Put them in a saucepan and stir in the butter, orange juice, zest and nutmeg.

Serves 8

Note: Boiled turnips may be enhanced with crispy fried shallots, parsley, cumin seeds or a little brown sugar.

TURNIP AND ONION GRATIN

Heat oven to 375 degrees.

> 1 pound turnips, peeled and grated
> 1 onion, finely chopped
> 3 teaspoons cornstarch
> 1/2 cup grated Parmesan
> 2/3 cup heavy cream
> salt and pepper to taste

Toss the onions and turnips with the cornstarch, 1/4 cup of the Parmesan, salt and pepper in a bowl. Transfer the mixture to a 9 x 12 casserole or baking tin, patting it down. Drizzle the cream over the mixture, then the remaining Parmesan. Bake in the middle of the oven for 25 or 30 minutes until the top is golden.

Serves 4

ZUCCHINI

Zucchini and squash, like eggplant, are inclined to exude moisture while being cooked. The same treatment—salting the slices and draining—helps a lot.

A cup of rice may be added to this dish, and some Parmesan, too.

ZUCCHINI AND SQUASH

>3 yellow squash
>3 zucchini
>8 scallions
>7 tablespoons olive oil
>Our Special Salt

Cut the end off the squash and the zucchini and then slice them, once vertically and then across in thin slices. Put them in a colander, salting every handful or so. They should drain for about two hours. If they taste too salty, rinse them with cold water and drain.

Slice the scallions, some of the green part, too.

Heat the olive oil in a large wok or deep skillet. Add the vegetables and stir fry with two wooden spoons. This will take about ten minutes.

Serve with lots of Our Special Salt.

You might want to add a couple of cups of cooked rice to this.

Serves 4

GRILLED ZUCCHINI

> **5 or 6 zucchini**
> **1/4 cup olive oil**
> **juice of 1 lemon**
> **1/2 cup thinly sliced fresh basil**
> **Our Special Salt**

Trim the ends of zucchini and slice lengthwise into 1/4 inch strips.

Dip them in oil, coating well, and fry them on a hot griddle over medium heat, turning frequently, until they are soft and scorched with griddle marks.

Pasta and Rice

$\mathcal{T}$hin and thick, curly and straight, seashells and bow ties, noodles and macaroni—there are more than 400 kinds of pasta from which to choose. Meat, fish, vegetable and cheese sauces abound.

BOW TIES WITH PEAS AND MINT

> 1/2 pound bow tie pasta
> large saucepan boiling water
> 1/2 cup heavy cream
> mint leaves, cut narrowly (julienne)
> 1/2 teaspoon lemon zest
> 1/2 cup cooked peas, fresh or frozen
> Our Special Salt
> 1/2 cup grated parmesan cheese

Cook pasta about ten minutes, until al dente.

Put in large serving bowl and add peas, mint, lemon zest, cream, salt and butter. Toss, and sprinkle Parmesan cheese on top.

FETTUCCINE, SPAGHETTI AND LINGUINE

These are good with vegetables and cheese. Often served with a good pesto, here are some recipes.

BLENDER PESTO

> 2 cups fresh basil, leaves only
> 3 minced garlic cloves
> 1 cup pine nuts
> 3/4 cup olive oil

Process basil, garlic and nuts until well chopped. With blender on, add oil in a stream until blended. Store in refrigerator or freezer.

ANOTHER BLENDER PESTO

> 1 cup parsley
> 1/2 cup basil
> 1 tablespoon thyme or tarragon
> 1/2 cup grated Parmesan
> 1/3 cup olive oil
> 1 tablespoon balsamic vinegar

Process parsley, herbs, and cheese; then add oil and vinegar.

HANDMADE PESTO

big bunch of stemmed parsley
big bunch watercress
6 large garlic cloves
3 tablespoons basil
1/2 cup parmesan cheese
Our Special Salt and pepper
1 1/2 olive oil

Chop fine the parsley, watercress and basil, preferably in a wooden bowl. Press garlic and then pound in a mortar with olive oil. add to bowl. Mix in cheese, salt and pepper and lots of oil.

You could serve the pasta hot and let the guests scoop out a big spoonful of this sauce on top.

ANCHOVY PESTO

This is good on almost any pasta. For those little shaped pasta you might have to double the recipe.

2 cans anchovy filet
2 tablespoons Parmesan cheese
equal parts butter (or oil)

Mix well.

MACARONI RING

Heat oven to 350 degrees.

Macaroni is baked as often as it is boiled, and usually served with cheese. It also lends itself to rings or loafs.

> 3/4 cup macaroni
> 3 tablespoons melted butter
> 1/2 cup cream
> 3 eggs
> 1/2 cup grated cheese
> 1/4 cup chopped canned green chilies
> 1 tablespoon grated raw onion

Boil the macaroni for about ten minutes, drain and put in a bowl.

Scald the cream and beat the eggs into it. Pour the butter over the macaroni.

Combine all the ingredients and pat down into a buttered ring mold. Bake for about an hour.

Serve with creamed mushrooms or a creamed vegetable.

RICE

BASMATI RICE WITH RAISINS

       3/4 cup golden raisins
       4 sliced scallions
       1/2 cup white wine
       3 tablespoons butter
       3 1/2 cups beef broth
       1/4 cup lightly toasted pine nuts
       1 1/2 cup basmati rice

Soak the raisins in the wine for ten minutes. Heat butter in pot, stir in rice for five minutes. add wine, scallions, broth. Cook covered on a low simmer for 20-25 minutes. Sprinkle pine nuts on top of rice when serving.

ORANGE RICE

1/4 cup butter
2 tablespoons chopped onions
3/4 cup chopped celery
1 1/2 tablespoon grated orange rind
1 1/2 cups orange juice
1 teaspoon salt
1/8 teaspoon nutmeg
1 cup rice
1 cup water
1/3 cup slivered blanched almonds

Sauté onion and celery in butter in a 3 quart saucepan, about 5 minutes. Add orange juice, orange peel, water, salt and nutmeg and bring to boiling. Slowly stir in rice cook covered over low heat about 25 minutes. Add almonds before serving.

MUSHROOM RISOTTO

"They" say that one must watch risotto carefully the whole time it is cooking, adding boiling stock bit by bit until it is absorbed and the rice is done. This takes about 20 minutes standing by the stove, ignoring your guests and growing increasingly bored.

This mushroom risotto does not require constant care.

> 6 tablespoons butter
> 3 tablespoons olive oil
> 1/4 pound
> 2/3 cup Arborio rice
> 2/3 cup white wine
> 1 1/4 cup vegetable stock
> 1/4 cup grated parmesan cheese

Melt the oil and half the butter and add mushrooms, letting them let cook gently for a few minutes.

Add rice (and a pinch of saffron if you have it), mix and let the rice soak up the juices; then add wine, seasonings and stock. Bring to a boil and simmer, covered, for 8 minutes, Remove from heat and let stand for five minutes. Stir in remaining butter, melted, and the cheese.

RISOTTO WITH CELERY etc.

Don't be intimidated by risotto!

You can make up your own version, using Arborio rice. Chopped celery always adds a wonderful flavor. You might add some peas, maybe a few asparagus sprigs, a few mushrooms etc etc etc. You can use chicken, vegetable beef stock or wine. I once had risotto made with red wine.

Chop the celery and any other vegetables. Heat the stock and keep it just under a boil during this procedure. Melt some butter, add it and the rice, simmer gently. Add vegetables and about a half cup of stock. Let this come to a nice simmer for a few minutes; when it is absorbed add a whole cup of stock, and let it simmer while you busy yourself with other chores.

It's hard to tell how much liquid the rice will take; you are going to have to play this by ear. Inspect the rice and taste it. Done, no? Add more stock gradually. Done, yes? Cover and let it sit.

Add more butter and seasonings before serving. You might top it with crispy bacon bits or bits of fried chicken livers, anything goes!

SAFFRON RICE

Saffron must be one if the most expensive spices in the world. Fortunately a small pinch does wonders.

> 3/4 cup white wine
> 3/4 teaspoon crumbled saffron threads
> 3 tablespoons butter
> 2 1/2/ cups long grain rice
> 3 3/4 cups chicken broth

Melt butter in saucepan over medium heat; add onion and sauté until soft. Add rice and stir five minutes. Add wine and stir in saffron, simmer and stir about five minutes, until evaporated.

Add broth and bring to a boil, then reduce heat and simmer, covered, about 18 minutes until done. Season and serve.

WILD RICE

Because it is so difficult to harvest, wild rice remains a sort of luxury food. Onions and mushrooms are almost vital for a good wild rice dish. Combined with brown or white rice it goes farther and is quite nice.

> 1/2 cup wild rice
> 1/2 cup white or brown rice
> 4 cups water or stock
> 4 tablespoons butter
> 2 onions, minced
> 1/2 pound mushrooms, chopped
> 1 teaspoon salt

Rinse the rice well in several waters.

Bring water and salt to a boil, add the rice slowly, and cook, uncovered, about 40 minutes or more.

Sauté onion and mushrooms in 2 tablespoons butter while rice is cooking.

When rice is done, stir in the remaining butter, mushrooms and onions.

Desserts

$\mathcal{I}$rma Rombauer of the *Joy of Cooking* once said that to describe the beating of an egg white was almost as cheeky as advising how to live a happy life.

But as so many of our deserts call for stiffly beaten egg whites we must remind you: a very clean bowl and very clean beaters are vital for success.

BREAD PUDDING

The late Patricia Moore, a long time resident of Aspen, Colorado, gave me this recipe about ten years ago and I have copied it here exactly as she wrote it.

When she died a few years ago, her friend John McBride was designated to distribute her ashes from his small plane. He and Billy Hunt flew over Aspen and decided that since she loved the Little Nell Hotel, that would be a good place to drop the ashes. Unfortunately, many of them blew down on the guests having lunch outside on the Hotel's terrace. And, even more unfortunately, it was the day after the big anthrax scare.

Pat would have loved it all.

Set oven to 325 degrees.

> 7 slices bread (I use the thick Pepperidge Farm kind and cut off the crusts)
> a quart of milk
> 3 eggs, slightly beaten
> 1/2 cup sugar (I prefer brown, which I don't always have)
> 1 1/2 tsp salt
> 1/2 cup raisins
> 1 tsp vanilla (she says optional; I say essential)
> 1/2 tsp cinammon (she says optional, I say DO IT)

Butter a two-quart baking dish (I forgot today and often do). Butter one side of each slice of bread and sides of them, (I just put them in the dish...bottom, of course and then piled up—could that be wrong?) Pour the mixed stuff over, press bread down. Let stand if bread is dry. Bake covered for 30 minutes, and uncovered for 30 minutes more. Under the broiler if you want it browner and crustier.

Comes from oven puffy and then falls slowly. She (aha! A Mrs. Cunningham) says heavy cream—I have used the phony Cool Whip and ice cream. I do eat rather a lot of it.

COFFEE SOUFFLE

Soufflés are not hard to make, and this one is light and lovely.

One evening I was watching "Emeril Live," my favorite program on the Food Channel, and he put his fallen soufflé back into the oven. It did, indeed, rise up again! I must remember to try it.

Sauce:

> 1 cup heavy cream
> 4 large egg yolks, beaten
> 1 teaspoon vanilla

Put the beaten egg yolks in a pan. Scald the cream in another pan, pour over egg yolks and set over medium heat for a minute. Let it cool and add the vanilla.

Soufflé:

Heat oven to 375 degrees.

> 6 large egg whites
> 1 1/8 cup sugar
> 1 1/2 teaspoon powdered coffee
> 1 teaspoon cocoa
> 5 drops mocha flavoring

Butter a 7 1/2 inch soufflé dish and shake sugar in it.

Beat the egg whites (remember: clean beaters, clean bowl!) until stiff. Sift the sugar, coffee and cocoa, and add slowly to the egg whites, beating it to a stiff meringue. Add the mocha extract. Put mixture into dish, set dish into a pan with about an inch of hot water, and bake 15 minutes at 375; then turn oven to 325 and bake 10 or 25 minutes more.

Serves 6

APPLE TARTE

From my friend, Francie Dye, a very good cook, comes this idiotically simple tarte.

> **frozen pie crust**
> **2 cans apples**
> **cinnamon**

Put crust in tart pan, add a dash of cinnamon to one or two cans of apples, fold pastry edges over the filling and bake as directed on crust package.

You can also use canned pears, peaches, frozen berries…or if you have time, fresh fruit. Jazz it up with Cool Whip or real whipped cream.

Serves 6

HEALTHY PIE

I didn't think it was seemly to call this "Heart Attack Pie" but it does stem from the time that Max Goracke of Snowmass Village, Colorado had a heart attack. He loved sweets, and this is the pie that his wife, Pat, concocted for him out of fairly harmless ingredients. It's delectable, too.

Heat oven to 375 degrees.

> **3 egg whites**
> **1 teaspoon cream of tartar**
> **6 crumbled soda crackers**
> **1/2 cup chopped pecans**
> **1 teaspoon vanilla**

Beat egg whites, cream of tartar and sugar until stiff. Fold in crackers, oatmeal, pecans, and vanilla. Bake in a 9-inch greased pan, for 25 minutes.

Serves 6

MERINGUES

"You made it?" says the astonished guest, on being presented with a meringue filled with ice cream and topped with sauce. It has taken the hostess about eight minutes to prepare, but for some reason a meringue has about it an aura of culinary mystery. Actually it is one of the easiest deserts (or cookies) to produce.

Heat the oven to 275 degrees if you want the meringue to be a little stiff and crunchy or 225 degrees for a chewy meringue. You may also opt for overnight meringues—here the oven is heated to 475 degrees and turned off completely when the meringues are set in for their overnight stay.

> **4 egg whites at room temperature**
> **1 cup sugar**
> **1/2 teaspoon cream of tartar**
> **3 tablespoons cocoa (optional)**
> **brown paper cut from grocery bags**

In a clean glass bowl beat the egg whites with a clean electric beater till foamy, then add cream of tartar. Continue to beat until eggs hold very stiff peaks; add the sugar slowly and continue to beat until sugar is completely incorporated.

To make it miraculously easy to remove meringues from the pan, line it with brown paper cut from grocery bags. It is fool proof.

Now you may either make a large meringue layer, eight or nine individual nests, or dozens of cookies.

For nests, put large spoonfuls of the mixture onto the paper, and spread out until it is about four inches in diameter, Poke down the center, and build up the edges with more paste.

The recipe will make one large meringue about nine inches in diameter; spread the paste onto the paper and mold up the edges.

If you decide to try cookies, perhaps you might add to the mixture a cup of coconut, or a cup of, yes, Rice Krispies, or some chopped ginger. Drop the mixture by tablespoons onto the paper. You might need another pan.

After any these meringues have baked for an hour, test them to see if they can be easily removed from the paper. If not, bake fifteen minutes more. Then turn off the heat, letting the meringues rest in the oven for a while. Peel them gently off the paper. The overnight meringues are removed in the morning.

You may fill the nests or the large meringue with ice cream and chocolate sauce or sliced raspberries or strawberries. Maybe some whipped cream?

Applause

OUR SECRET CUSTARD

Call this flan, crème caramel, crème renversee or what you
will…it is actually Jell-O Americana Pudding Mix, enhanced
a little.

> **1 package Jell-O Americana Pudding mix**
> **3 cups whole milk**
> **1 egg**
> **3/4 cup sugar**

While preparing pudding mix according to package
directions, (adding the egg), melt the sugar in a small heavy
skillet, stirring slightly. It should be ready at the same time
as the pudding, First pour the sugar into a serving dish or
mold, trying to dribble some down the sides; then pour the
hot pudding on top. Chill and serve to glowing comments.

196

PINEAPPLE BITES

> 1 fresh pineapple
> 1 cup sour cream
> 1 cup brown sugar

Put bite-size pieces of pineapple into a shallow glass bowl, slather with sour cream and cover with brown sugar. Chill for two hours and serve.

SEMIFREDDO

Another recipe from Alex Gancarz: this one for an Italian "semi-frozen" desert is simpler than it might sound. Not many of my guests have ever tasted it before. Compliments abound!

> **10 1/2 oz white chocolate chips, or chopped white chocolate**
> **3 eggs at room temperature, separated**
> **1 cup well chilled heavy cream**
> **3 tablespoon sugar**
> **2 tablespoons Amaretto (or vanilla)**
> **Thawed frozen raspberries or strawberries for sauce.**

Line a 9 x 5 metal loaf pan with plastic wrap, leaving a generous overhang at the ends, and chill in freezer.

Get out a double boiler and three large glass bowls. Melt the chocolate in the double boiler over hot (not boiling) water, stirring well until very smooth. Let this cool to lukewarm.

Beat the whites until they hold nice stiff peaks. Beat the cream until it holds stiff peaks. Mix egg yolks, sugar and Amaretto until the mixture is thick.

Now fold the egg whites into the cream thoroughly, cutting through with a rubber spatula.

Next fold half the chocolate into the yolk mixture, then add a fourth of the cream/egg white mixture, folding gently but thoroughly.

Then fold in the remaining chocolate and the remaining cream/egg white mixture.

Pour it all into the chilled pan, cover with plastic wrap, and let freeze for at least 8 hours or overnight. It is easy to unmold onto a platter by pulling on the overlapping ends. Let it sit for a few minutes, then slice with a sharp knife, and serve with the following sauce.

SAUCE

Alex's sauce calls for strawberries pureed in a blender with three tablespoons sugar and a fourth cup Amoretto. But thawed berries alone are almost as good.

Serves 8

STRAWBERRIES WITH PEPPER

This sounds like a really strange combination, but it is always a total success.

> 2 pints strawberries
> 1/2 stick melted butter
> 1 cup sugar
> 1/2 cup orange juice
> 3 tablespoons cracked (not just coarse, but
>   cracked black pepper
> whipped cream

Large strawberries may be cut in half.

Make a sauce by boiling butter, sugar and orange juice for three minutes in a large skillet. This may be done ahead of time. Add the strawberries to the skillet when you are ready to serve and heat them in the sauce for three minutes, sprinkle with pepper and serve topped with whipped cream.

Serves 8

TREACLE TART

An English friend, Elizabeth Henderson, one of the best cooks I know, gave me this recipe. She is the mother of the famous London chef and restaurateur, Fergus Henderson. I think he would probably agree that a lot of his success is due to her example in the kitchen.

This delectable desert is very rich and needs no cream or sauce. (Elizabeth would scorn my "boughten" piecrust.)

Heat oven to 375 degrees.

> **2 defrosted frozen piecrusts**
> **1 pound can Lyle's Golden Syrup**
> **1/2 stick butter**
> **2 eggs, beaten**
> **1 large lemon, zest and juice**
> **6 oz breadcrumbs**

Put the two packaged pastry crusts on top of each other and roll out with some vigor to make one large crust to line a 12-inch tart pan. Fold any extra crust onto rim of tin.

Warm the Golden Syrup in a heavy pan over moderate heat. Remove from heat and stir in the butter. While it melts mix eggs, lemon juice, zest, and breadcrumbs. Combine ingredients and tip mixture into pan; bake for 30 minutes.

Serves 8

Cookies

$\mathcal{A}$ new word describing cookie-lovers: opsomaniacs! It comes from "opso: rich fare and mania: exaggerated desire for." So the opsomaniac has a morbid longing for dainties like the following goodies.

OPSOMANIA: A Morbid Longing For Dainties

KATHARINE'S OATMEAL COOKIES

My oldest friend, Katharine Kunhardt, and I have been struggling with these no-flour cookies for years. They are astonishingly good…when they work and you can peel them right off the cookie sheet…but too often the whole procedure is a disaster.

Maybe she has given up spending any time in the kitchen, for she has written a book *Count the Puppies* with pictures of some of her Westorchard Labrador litters. Her husband, Phil , former managing editor of LIFE Magazine, has a new book, too, *The Dreaming Game*. It's about his mother, Dorothy, author of *Pat the Bunny* among her other children's books.

To get back to the cookies: now I have a real non-stick cookie sheet and all is well. I suppose a Silpat cover would work, too?

Heat oven 350 degrees.

> **1 stick butter, melted**
> **1 cup sugar**
> **1 cup brown sugar**
> **2 cups oatmeal**
> **3 eggs beaten**
> **2 teaspoons vanilla**

Mix everything together and place small teaspoonfuls on an ungreased baking sheet. Bake for about ten minutes, inspecting after about seven minutes for doneness.

One is supposed to leave on the cookie sheet for a minute or two, then hurry, hurry and get them off with a spatula. Good luck!.

SPRINGERLE

These cookies were a Christmas delight of my childhood when we went to my grandmother's house. After she died there were many years without Springerle when, behold, I found this recipe in the *Joy Of Cooking*. I have adapted it slightly.

If you do not have any of the wooden molds or a special rolling pin used to stamp designs on these cookies, just cut the dough into 1 x 2 inch bars; the taste will be the same. Or maybe you can find something to press on the dough to make a design.

I have doubled this recipe a few times for myself, but this makes a massive amount of dough to cope with.

These cookies are made, rolled, stamped and cut one day and baked the next.

> **4 eggs**
> **2 cups sugar**
> **3 to 3 1/2 cups flour**
> **1/2 teaspoon baking powder**
> **2 tablespoons crushed anise seed**

Beat the eggs and sift the sugar into them gradually. then beat until creamy.

Sift flour with baking powder, and sprinkle a cup of this onto a pastry cloth (or a countertop). Add the sugar/egg mixture, kneading in more flour until the dough is really thick. Roll it out to about a half inch and press the floured wooden mold on it hard to get a good imprint. If the dough sticks, add more flour.

Cut the squares and let them dry on breadboards overnight. (Your un-imprinted cookies must dry as well).

The next day, when ready to bake:

Heat oven to 300 degrees.

Heavily butter cookie sheets and sprinkle them with anise seed which you have crushed with a rolling pin, Place the cakes on the tins and bake fifteen minutes, until the lower part is light yellow.

Store in a tin or glass jar.

SUGAR COOKIES

Don't ask, don't tell, about these cookies, They are straight from the frozen section at your grocery, rolled out in your kitchen, sliced or cut into fancy shapes, sprinkled with colored sugar, and baked. Eureka!

TOLL HOUSE MADE BETTER

Munching away in the kitchen of Susie and Peter Kunhardt in Chappaqua, his mother and father and I went through an awful lot of these cookies one Sunday afternoon.

"Toll House," said Susie, but the secret to their goodness was the omission of a cup and a half of the flour called for on the package recipe. Try it!

Thanksgiving Made Easy

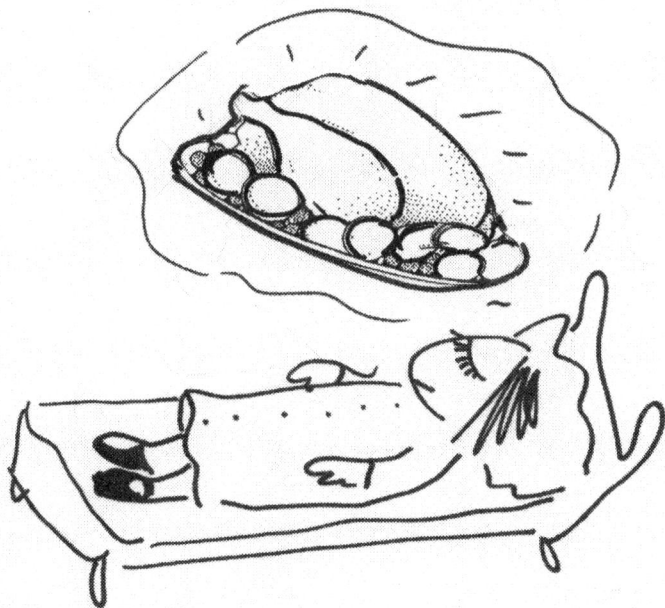

TURKEY

Many years ago, Stella Standard, author of many cookbooks and a friend of my mothers, told us that the best (and easiest) way to cook a turkey was in a brown paper sack. My family has been doing it this way ever since. It requires no basting, browns beautifully, exudes juices for gravy, and is always satisfactory.

Preheat oven to 350 degrees.

Have on hand a large brown paper bag, the kind your groceries come in.

> **12 to 18 pound turkey**
> **1/2 cup melted butter**
> **stuffing (see recipe)**

Remove neck, giblets, and liver (save this for gravy if you like) from the turkey, and then stuff it as usual. With a brush, generously cover turkey with butter. Carefully put the turkey in the bag (it is easier if someone helps by holding the bag open). Twist the end and place it on a rack in a roasting pan. Cook for 18-20 minutes to the pound; for a bird over 18 pounds 13 to 15 minutes a pound is enough. Unstuffed birds require less cooking time, and most people cook turkeys longer than necessary.

When it's done remove the paper and there it is: a beautifully browned unbasted turkey! Put the bird on a platter to "rest" for about ten minutes before carving while you prepare some gravy.

GRAVY

> 3 tablespoons pan juices
> 3 tablespoons flour
> 1 cup chicken stock
> salt and pepper

Skim off the fat in the roasting pan; reserve 3 tablespoons of pan juices, add three tablespoons flour and stir until blended and golden. Slowly add cup of stock, blending as you go. Add the liver, chopped, if you want.

STUFFING, or more elegantly, DRESSING

Pepperidge Farm or any of the other packaged stuffings are good basic stuffings that you may jazz up with sautéed chopped turkey livers, some chopped onion, sautéed mushrooms, a few chestnuts, or whatever. But it is perfectly good made following the recipe on the bag.

MAGICAL CRANBERRY SAUCE

2 cans cranberries, either whole or jellied or mixed

Pour the cranberries into a heavy saucepan and stir until they melt completely. Pour into a mold; chill. When unmolded over a little hot water this will look like a photograph from a gourmet food magazine.

CREAMED ONIONS

Look for onions canned in a glass jar…they serve nicely for this dish.

> **2 cans small onions**
> **3 tablespoons butter**
> **3 tablespoons flour**
> **3/4 cup half and half or milk**
> **1/4 cup onion liquid**
> **1 teaspoon grated nutmeg**

Drain the onions, reserving 1/4 cup liquid.

Make a cream sauce by melting the butter, stirring in the flour and slowly adding the cream and onion liquid, blending as you do so. Add nutmeg. The sauce should be rather thick.

In a serving bowl gently mix the onions and the sauce.

STUFFED CELERY

Perhaps this was an Omaha tradition, or maybe just a family quirk, but we always had stuffed celery at Christmas. Even as children we liked this Roquefort version.

celery hearts
Roquefort or blue cheese
a little mayonnaise
paprika

Mix the mayonnaise with the cheese and stuff the celery sticks, adding a dash of paprika for color.

Index

www.ingramcontent.com/pod-product-compliance
Lightning Source LLC
Chambersburg PA
CBHW031250090426
42742CB00007B/390